JUVENILE COURT AND COMMUNITY CORRECTIONS

Thomas G. Blomberg

School of Criminology
Florida State University

UNIVERSITY
PRESS OF
AMERICA

LANHAM • NEW YORK • LONDON

ISBN (Perfect): 0-8191-4261-1
ISBN   (Cloth): 0-8191-4260-3

All University Press of America books are produced on acid-free
paper which exceeds the minimum standards set by the National
Historical Publications and Records Commission.

ACKNOWLEDGEMENTS

In developing this book, I have become indebted to several persons and agencies. I want to acknowledge the excellent help extended by personnel of the county juvenile court that I studied and personnel of the California Youth Authority's Division of Research and Development. Sherry Caraballo assisted ably in the collection and analysis of the study's data. Edwina Ivory generously provided typing services. Jerome Skolnick provided suggestions for improving the early manuscript.

I am especially indebted to Sheldon Messinger for his criticisms, thoughtful recommendations, and support throughout the course of this work. If not for his suggestion, the study would not have been undertaken.

And finally, I am indebted as always to my wife, Jeanine Blomberg, who contributed to each phase of the research and writing of this book.

TABLE OF CONTENTS

LIST OF FIGURE AND TABLES

Figure

Table

PREFACE

During the past several decades, community corrections have provided a major thrust in dealing with juvenile delinquency. Underlying the community corrections movement has been an attempt to get away from the use of institutions and the formal juvenile court system by providing troubled youths with various community corrections alternatives which have been assumed to be more effective. Like other reforms in other epochs, community corrections has been hailed by its proponents as the modern savior of youth. To date, however, the degree to which various community correctional efforts for youths are successful remains questionable.

This book assesses the community corrections experiences of a California juvenile court and associated experiences nationwide. The study aims in part, to question the conventional wisdom by providing an empirical assessment of these experiences which is sensitive to the potential of community correctional reforms to produce unintended consequences. Among the major findings is documentation of the unintended consequence of "net-widening," a situation in which community correctional reforms are shown to increase rather than to alter the juvenile court's reach and its control over youths and, in many instances, their families.

Today, the phenomenon of net-widening continues to grow at an alarming rate. It is being furthered not only by the juvenile court and community corrections, but by the overall justice system and various federal, state, and local government agencies concerned with welfare, mental health, and education. This means that a larger proportion of this country's population is now subject to some form of state intervention and control than in any previous period.

This Orwellian <u>1984</u> scenario, or what has been termed the coming of a "minimum security society," poses several dilemmas. One of these is that increased state intervention brought on by net-widening reduces individual freedom and produces other damaging effects on clients. These include increased numbers of rearrests, family disintegration, and other related behavior difficulties. Yet in direct contrast to these damaging effects, state intervention can also produce various social and client benefits related to reducing subsequent crime and other forms of human suffering. Unfortunately, we do not yet know clearly what specific reform programs can and cannot do for various clients or what effect they will have on social concerns. Given the potential these reform programs have for producing disparate results, it is difficult not to be ambivalent about them. Yet such ambivalence, while understandable, does not provide the basis necessary for establishing sound correctional reform policies.

This book addresses these program reform issues by considering some examples generated from a jurisdiction's community correctional reform movement for youths and by examining the nationwide implications of those examples. It assesses both the dangers inherant in various correctional reforms and their beneficial potential, and identifies an evaluation approach capable of differentiating between these two kinds of potential to inform future policies.

Two central arguments will be developed in the study. First, the organizational character of the juvenile court facilitates implementation of community correctional reforms as service supplements rather than as alternatives, which results in net-widening. Second, all correctional reforms are subject to drift because of various impediments to their implementation; nonetheless it is possible to evaluate the implementation process to determine what is possible--and impossible--for reform programs and services to do and who they can affect when they have been implemented in order to provide a guide for responsible correctional policy-making.

CHAPTER 1

INTRODUCTION

HISTORICAL OVERVIEW

During the course of American history, several distinct strategies have been employed to control criminal and delinquent behavior. Colonial Americans, for example, did not view crime as a major social problem, and therefore expended little time or energy in crime control or offender rehabilitation. In fact, Colonial Americans were at times very forgiving with offenders, by giving them another chance, and at other times very callous and cruel in their infliction of severe punishments on offenders.

Toward the end of the 18th century, Colonial crime control strategies began to decline with the increasing ideological influences of the Enlightenment and Classical criminology. Specifically, between 1790 and 1830, Americans began to shift from the "grim determinism" that had characterized Colonial thought toward a new optimism which emphasized mankind's ability to respond effectively to crime. Under the free will ideology of the Classical School, Americans put their crime control energies into effective law enforcement and swift and sure adjudication to control and deter crime.

During 1830, various social, political, economic, and intellectual changes led to another shift in crime causation theory and associated strategies of control. Jacksonian Americans viewed crime as resulting from an increasingly disorganized social environment that was associated with industrialization and urbanization. This thinking led to what Rothman has termed "the discovery of the asylum."[1]

Various institutions were created to counter the ill effects of the disorganized urban environment. The prevalent thinking was that an institutional environment free of corruption could rid the individual of the negative traits nurtured by the urban setting and ultimately provide individuals, upon release from the institution, with a "spiritual coat of armor" that would shield them from the rampant sin, vice, and corruption in the urban setting.[2]

In the 1850s, it was reasoned that prisons were not fulfilling their function of changing people, and that alternative correctional strategies were needed. During this period, youth reformatories, parole, and probation reforms developed as alternatives to previous prison policies. By the turn of the twentieth century, the juvenile court was being implemented and hailed as the ultimate reform step in the humanitarian and progressive treatment of delinquency. From 1900 until the 1950s, juvenile correction reforms were centered upon differentiating, refining, and proliferating reformatory, parole, probation, and juvenile court strategies.

Beginning in the 1950s, nationwide attention was focused on the development of alternative community-based correction services for troubled youths. During the early stages of the community correction movement, local institutions, residential centers, group homes, and specialized probation services were promoted as alternatives to placing youths in state reformatories.

In the late 1960s, a second phase of the community correction movement stimulated an explosion of diversion and deinstitutionalization programs that were promoted as alternatives to the juvenile court and local and state institutions. What underlay the community correction movement was the widely held belief that state reformatories and the juvenile court system had failed. In fact, they were viewed as having produced more harm than good by stigmatizing youths and subjecting them to damaging delinquent associations, thereby accelerating delinquency.

Until the 1970s, literature on community corrections was similar to earlier literature on traditional corrections (i.e., institutions, parole, and probation). It was largely descriptive, theoretical, or exhortatory and without meaningful empirical interests. Moreover, the evaluation studies of community correctional programs that appeared in the early 1970s reported results that were uneven, contradictory, and as Hylton suggests, limited in two other important respects.[3] First, the studies did not produce conclusive results about the overall value of community correctional programs. Second, impact or effectiveness was approached so narrowly that confusion remained. In effect, characteristic evaluations of community corrections were focused upon determining only the recidivism impact these programs were producing while ignoring other effects of the programs on youths and impacts on the system. This narrow evaluation orientation produced limited results and contributed to what can now be described as an incomplete understanding of community correctional programs.

The implementation of community correctional programs as it was officially promoted, was to result in reduced use of state reformatories and other preexisting juvenile court strategies by providing troubled youths alternative forms of community treatment, thereby reducing their likelihood of subsequent delinquent behavior. It was assumed that the programs would be implemented according to their conceptual rationale as

2

alternatives to previous court practices. Unfortunately, such an assumption was not necessarily warranted.

There are a number of impediments in the way of appropriate program implementation that can shape, modify, and even subvert reform efforts. Klein identifies several impediments characteristic of the implementation of youth correction reforms. These include poorly developed program rationales, inappropriately selected groups of youths, narrowly conceived treatment and service strategies, professional resistance to reform efforts, and placement of the programs in inappropriate settings.[4] Ultimately, how the juvenile court responds to and implements correction reforms substantially shapes the outcomes produced by the programs. While well conceived and clearly articulated correction reforms have greater likelihood of appropriate implementation, they remain susceptible to subversion during implementation of their programs. Unfortunately, the potential for program modification during implementation has been largely ignored in previous studies of the juvenile court's experiences with community correction reforms.

Clearly, there is a need to know: (1) how the juvenile court responds to and implements various reforms; (2) the characteristic impacts produced by the court's implementation of these reforms; and (3) the policy implications posed by the impacts of the reform. This study addresses this need. The purposes are: (1) to describe a juvenile court's response to and implementation of three community correction reforms; (2) to document how the court's pattern of response and program implementation of these reforms results in net-widening, whereby the court's youth and related client reach are extended instead of altered; and (3) to consider an evaluation approach capable of differentiating the beneficial and detrimental result and impact capabilities of correction reforms for future policies.

The following two major arguments will be developed in the study. First, juvenile court organizations are characterized by operational uncertainty and opportunism which facilitates a blurring of the distinction between the court's organization and youth treatment needs. This results in the implementation of reforms as supplements rather than alternatives to previous court practice, thereby producing net-widening. Second, while all correction reforms are subject to program implementation impediments and drift, it is possible to evaluate the implementation process to determine what various programs and services, once implemented, can and cannot do and for whom to guide responsible policy-making.

3

Previous study of the juvenile court has been largely concentrated in four general categories. The orientations of these studies are progressive, legal, theoretical, and empirical. The progressive works tend to view the court as a positive legal reform and emphasize its humanitarian philosophy and individualized treatment goals. Representative studies are those by Boole, Chute, Dobbs, Garabedian and Gibbons, and Teeters and Reinneman.[5] The problems or inadequacies of the court, to the extent they are addressed, are explained by these writers as the result of failure to provide the court with necessary organizational resources.

A legal analysis of juvenile court law and proceedings is provided in the works by Allen, Arnold, Caldwell, Handler, Newman, Rosenheim, and Tappan.[6] These studies are concerned with the juvenile court's broadly delegated discretionary powers and the punitive potential of these powers. They provide support for a shift from the acceptance shown in the progressive works of the court's presumed "treatment" orientation to a realization of the punitive and nontherapeutic consequences that can result from broad discretionary powers, regardless of official treatment aims. Tappan, for example, cautions that unless the juvenile court judge

> be circumscribed in some degree by established instrumental or traditional rule and form, the fate of the defendant, the interest of society, and the social objectives themselves must hang by the tenuous thread of the wisdom and personality of the particular administration.[7]

Such concerns provided a basis for restructuring the juvenile court procedures along more adversarial lines, culminating with the U.S. Supreme Court decision of Kent v. U.S. (1966) and In re Gault (1967).

More recent studies have displayed particular theoretical and associated empirical interest in juvenile court operations. The interests have reflected the emergence of labeling theory. As summarized by Ward, the two basic assumptions of labeling theory are: (1) social control agencies, such as the police and juvenile courts, categorize youths according to such criteria as race, dress, and demeanor and then focus attention on them and (2) by this process these agencies stimulate a commitment to subsequent delinquent behavior.[8] For example, it has been shown in investigating these assumptions that police, juvenile court intake, and disposition decisions are associated with such offender characteristics as race, family status, and demeanor.[9]

However, individual critiques of these works by Hagan, Ward, and Wellford have contended that the studies have been of questionable rigor and analytical sophistication.[10] Moreover, there are several studies that have shown police and court intake and disposition decisions to be more closely related to the nature of the offense, degree of damage associated with the offense, and prior offense record, than to offender characteristics.[11]

Organizational interest in juvenile court operations has emerged in studies by Cicourel and Emerson.[12] These works have focused upon selected court organization characteristics and tendencies in their attempts to validate labeling theory. Cicourel, for example, describes the need of court agents to generate an explanation of the behavior they encounter and to place the behavior in standard response categories that enable routine, expedient, and rational organizational processing of cases. Specifically, he argues in support of labeling theory that physical appearance, general demeanor, and non-offense-related variables provide a cause for the court's disposition of various youth cases.[13]

Emerson suggests that juvenile court decisions are influenced by both internal and external relations between the court and its institutional and political environment. He contends that juvenile court is characterized by a routine orientation shaped by the court's adaptation to its political and institutional environment. This environmental adaptation undermines the court's treatment concerns and results instead in control-related responses to youth cases that come before the court.[14]

In sum, the development of juvenile court inquiry has produced several traditions. Prior to labeling theory, court literature focused on descriptions of the court's humanitarian philosophy or on legal discussions of the court's broad discretionary powers. Interest in labeling theory stimulated theoretical and empirical study of juvenile court practices and initiated organizational interest in the juvenile court. Unfortunately, preoccupation with labeling theory has resulted in a narrow research focus aimed primarily at supporting or refuting the association between offender characteristics and corresponding court dispositions.

Studies focused specifically on the juvenile court as an organization are few. Clearly, there is a need to know more about juvenile court organizations, such as their characteristic structures, their processes, and their functional problems. In short, if reform efforts aimed at altering court practices are to have a fair opportunity, it is necessary to understand what juvenile courts are like as organizations.

JUVENILE COURTS AS ORGANIZATIONS:
A PERSPECTIVE

This study employs an organizational perspective in its analysis of a series of community correction reforms within a local California juvenile court.

A major theoretical view underlying this study's perspective on juvenile court organization is that of the "institutional school" of organization inquiry.[15] This approach is unique in its view of an organization as a "whole." According to this approach, specific processes such as individual or small group activity and leadership combine to form the whole of the organization and give it an identifiable character. The emphasis on organizations as wholes implies differences between organizations. Thus, studies using this approach tend to be case studies which have produced limited comparative findings. The case study approach usually analyzes the organization's past to explain how its present character has been shaped.[16] In reviewing the organizational development emphasis of this approach, Perrow explains:

> Because the interchange of structure and function goes on over time, a "natural history" of an organization is needed. We cannot understand current crises or competencies without seeing how they were shaped. The present is rooted in the past; no organization (and no man) is free to act as if the situation were de novo and the world a set of discrete opportunities ready to be seized upon at will.[17]

Consequently, the questions that guide this approach revolve around an organization's attempt to reach satisfactory accommodations with its environment over time. These accommodations can lead to changes in the organization's goals and character. Several researchers have written about a variety of organizations that have changed their goals in favor of the organization's growth or survival.[18] Sudnow, for example, focused on how a particular court handled its criminal cases. His findings indicated the public defender persuaded the defendant to plead guilty to a lesser charge following an agreement on the defendant's classification by the public defender and prosecutor. Sudnow found that this negotiated classification and the subsequent guilty plea were not directly related to the facts of the case. In describing the public defender's activities with the defendant, he states:

> From the outset, the P.D. attends to establishing the typical character of the case before him and thereby instituting

6

routinely employed reduction arrangements. The defendant's appearance--his race, demeanor, age, style of talk, way of attending to the occasion of his incarceration--provides the P.D. with the initial sense of his place in the social structure. Knowing only that the defendant is charged with section 459 (Burglary) of the penal code, the P.D. employs his conception of typical burglars against which the character of the present defendant is assessed.[19]

Defendants who refused the reduced charge in return for a guilty plea were placed in a different category. Special prosecutors strongly pursued their cases as punishment for lack of cooperation. While these classifications and routine responses allowed the court to handle its caseload efficiently, they detracted substantially from the court's goal of due process. Several writers have provided similar analyses of corrections with regard to the displacement of treatment goals in favor of punishment or control practices.[20]

Perrow provides an interesting overview of the institutional approach and claims the orientation's main contributions are in three areas.

First, emphasis on the organization as a whole supports the concept that there is a variety of organizations, but that the variety is not so extensive that organizations cannot be classified for certain purposes according to basic characteristics. In terms of autonomy, for example, some organizations are considerably autonomous while others are extremely dependent on several other groups, agencies, and so on. Perrow elaborates:

Large business and industrial organizations are largely autonomous, and for that reason leadership processes are presumably different, technology has more leeway, and bureaucratization is essential for efficiency. Prisons, mental hospitals, and many small welfare agencies exist to show that something is being done about some problems, but few care just what it is or how effective it is; those who control the organization's resources (legislators, religious boards, etc.) care only that the "something" should not involve scandals and should not cost too much. Here again, the environment for leadership, technology, and

7

structure will be different, and inventories,
elegant formal theories, and so on may miss
the point.[21]

The second contribution Perrow outlines is the possibility
that organizations take on a life of their own independent of
their formal purposes or of the wishes of those in control.
Selznick's distinction between "organization" and "institution" is
an attempt to conceptualize this process.[22] The difference is
between the rational, mechanical, and "no-nonsense" systems view
of organizations versus the responsive, adaptive,
natural-life-of-its-own concept applied to institutions.[23] While
neither of these positions adequately describes the workings and
character of most organizations, the organization-institution
distinction has important implications for understanding
organizations. For example, if the juvenile court organization is
viewed from a rational or mechanical systems view, a number of
predictions follow. For instance, it would be expected that the
juvenile court guided by youth treatment goals would respond by
implementing youth correction reforms in ways consistent with
their conceptual rationales to enhance their youth treatment
functions. In contrast, the emphasis of the institution model on
organizational adaptation and natural-life-of-its-own leads to
quite different predictions. In this case, it would be expected
that the juvenile court, guided not only by youth treatment goals
but by organizational needs related to survival, maintenance, and
expansion, could subvert reforms by blurring organizational needs
with youth treatment goals thereby producing results and impacts
not intended by those reforms.

Third, the environment emphasis makes a dominant contribution
to the institutional school. Detailed analysis of the interaction
between the organization and its environment provides the
organization's story. Through this process of interaction, the
organization grows, declines, or changes. Organizations must
continually adapt or improvise to keep in favor with their chief
sources of support. The organization's environment provides it
resources. The more successful the organization is in maintaining
its environmental relationships, the greater the likelihood that
it can fulfill its needs related to its survival, maintenance, and
growth.

However, the institutional school is lacking most in this
environmental area because there has not been a systematic
connection between the environment and the organization. Perrow
elaborates:

> Parts of the "environment" are seen as
> affecting organizations, but the organization
> is not seen as defining, creating, and
> shaping its environment. We live in an

8

"organizational society" the institutionalists routinely announce, but the significant environment of organizations is other organizations, and generally other organizations that share the same interest, definitions of reality, and power.[24]

Therefore, it would be inaccurate to describe an organization's role in its environment as solely adaptive. By necessity, organizations such as the juvenile court are concerned with their perceived needs and seek environmental support in accordance with those needs. Unfortunately, research on organizations has underestimated and understudied the ways an organization seeks support through environment interaction. One reason for this has been the failure to describe what constitutes the environment of organizations. Perrow's suggestion that the "significant environment" of organizations is other organizations with similar interests, provides helpful assistance in this regard.[25]

Several works have examined organizational relations in terms of exchange activity. This involves viewing organizational networks as systems of interdependent interests. According to Gore, formal organizations are embedded "in an environment of other organizations as well as in a complex of norms, values, and collectivities of the society."[26] Organizations and their environmental constituents are interdependent components of a larger system, and reflect their interdependence through exchange relationships. Exchange between organizations need not involve direct reciprocal activity; it can involve indirect activity whose purpose is the realization of each organization's goals. In the case of juvenile courts, for example, a number of exchange relations with other organizations are necessary. These can include not only officially connected agencies (such as police and state reformatories), but the Superior Court, local judges' committees, grand jury, juvenile justice commissions, League of Women Voters, Lawyers' Wives, Women's Auxiliary, and other citizen groups. The frequency with which the court interacts with these agencies varies, and the nature of exchange is not always obvious. Describing the variety of organizational exchange relations, Cole writes:

> Although mere interaction does not of necessity mean that exchange will occur, these social contacts lead to the development of relations in which the aim of each participant is to safeguard his own interest. Through the recognition of these interests exchanges may be developed which will benefit both partners.[27]

9

With regard to the safeguard of interests, "domain consensus" is required. When organizations interact and their functions are not obvious, consensus must be negotiated. Attempts to achieve at least minimal consensus are the basis for most organizational interaction. Levine and White contend that

> the processes of achieving domain consensus constitute much of the interaction between organizations. While they may not involve the immediate flow of elements, they are often necessary preconditions for exchange of elements, because without at least minimal domain consensus there can be no exchange among organizations.[28]

The effort to establish domain consensus, especially between the state and local levels, is well demonstrated in California's development of juvenile courts. Formal statutes attempt to establish consensus, but they fall short. There are patterns of negotiation and cooperation which have taken shape between state and local courts over jurisdiction, functions, receipt of resources, and so on. For example, there have been ongoing negotiations about a variety of issues that formal statues fail to delineate, in an effort to clarify the relationship between local juvenile courts and the State's California Youth Authority, which administers state reformatories and parole services.[29] The differences between the youth service functions of juvenile courts and the State Youth Authority system are not at all clear. The Youth Authority has far greater access to financial resources, and over the years has been able to secure a degree of consensus with juvenile courts by providing them with financial subsidies and technical services. State subsidies entail the state dispensing money to the courts in return the courts provide specific services, perform functions, or engage in practices directed toward achieving state goals. This exchange has facilitated a working relationship between the two jurisdictional levels with a reasonable amount of specialization and has helped limit duplication of services and functions. However, the negotiable character of the relationships between the state and local levels must be recognized to understand the nature of these relationships.

Similar exchange relationships exist between the court organization and those local agencies that constitute its significant environment. The relations of several state and local organizations with the juvenile court are displayed in Figure 1.1 (on next page). The structural context and the types of resources that flow between the court and these organizations vary and require specification. By definition, exchange between two organizations involves activity that has either actual or anticipated consequences for the realization of their respective

10

goals or objectives.[30] Exchange can take the form of either cooperation or bargaining. Cole points out that the difference between these forms hinges on the question, "Were the conditions for the transfer of resources negotiated?"[31]

In terms of cooperative exchange, each organization recognizes that it is in its interest to be involved in the transfer of resources with another organization without negotiation. It is understood that cooperation is productive for both parties. This type of exchange activity is reflected in normal working relations between the police and juvenile court in the routine processing of youths.

Figure 1.1

Selected Exchange Relations in
a Juvenile Court System

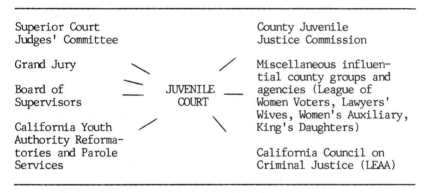

Superior Court
Judges' Committee

Grand Jury

Board of
Supervisors

California Youth
Authority Reforma-
tories and Parole
Services

JUVENILE
COURT

County Juvenile
Justice Commission

Miscellaneous influen-
tial county groups and
agencies (League of
Women Voters, Lawyers'
Wives, Women's Auxiliary,
King's Daughters)

California Council on
Criminal Justice (LEAA)

Exchange relations between two organizations which are characterized by bargaining involve the negotiation of conditions before the exchange of resources. This process occurs when representatives from each organization set the conditions for the exchange. For instance, the juvenile court's probation officer might meet with representatives of the Juvenile Justice Commission to discuss a needed expansion in court services.[32] The probation officer would attempt to persuade Commission representatives of the appropriateness of this expansion in order to gain their support and enlist their political influence with the Board of Supervisors for funding allocations. The Commission representatives, in turn, want to support changes that will reflect well on their organization and ease their operating problems. In order for an exchange to occur, there must be negotiations about the exchange that lead to some level of consensus between the two organizations. Cole points out that

11

bargaining of this nature "involves a strategy of compromise: a system of incentives by which all parties are brought to agree to the (final) settlement." [33]

Bargaining for exchange of resources between organizations is continual despite fairly dependable environment resources. Thompson and McEwen write in this regard:

> Even where fairly stable and dependable expectations have been built up with important elements of the organizational environment--with suppliers, distributors, legislators, workers, and so on--the organization cannot assume that these relationships will continue. Periodic review of these relationships must be accomplished, and an important means for this is bargaining, whereby each organization, through negotiation, arrives at a decision about future behavior satisfactory to the others involved.[34]

In the adjustment of relationships, organizations attempt to control their significant environments--namely, those organizations, groups, or individuals that have influence over their operation. An organization's attempt to gain environmental control can take a variety of forms aimed at initiating, maintaining, or strengthening environmental relations for eventual exchange. The extent of an organization's success in bargaining determines its access to resources. Resources available to an organization may also determine its success at bargaining. Access to resources provides the organization with effective means for realizing various goals. Therefore, from this perspective, it can be assumed that organizational goals, practices, and accomplishments are determined largely by ongoing political negotiations, compromises, and exchanges between organizations.

Functional Systems Studies

Studies of the justice system that have relied on various elements of the institutional school's orientation have been termed "functional systems studies." [35] These studies use the institutional model in varying degrees to describe justice agency processes and then to examine the causes for the observed processes. Functional systems studies have been centered upon the police and adult criminal courts.

According to Feeley, functional systems studies of the justice system have emphasized "the working conditions, the system of control, incentives and sanctions at the disposal of the

12

various actors, and the large environmental effects of the system."[36] Formal goals, rules, and defined roles are viewed as only one set of factors that shape and control justice agency practice. Other factors considered important include (1) ambiguity and multiplicity of goals, (2) external relations with various government units, private groups, and the general community, (3) internal relations with interrelated justice agencies, (4) conflicts between the quality of client handling and production requirements, and (5) operation within an environment characterized by resource scarcity and uncertainty.[37] While findings of these studies have varied, they can be summarized as pointing consistently to a disparity between everyday operations and official justice agency goals. In their attempts to explain the disparity between the goals of these agencies and their operations, functional systems analysts have focused on various combinations of the aforementioned organizational characteristics of these agencies.

Juvenile Court as an Organization

In this study's assessment of a juvenile court's experiences with community correction reforms, a functional systems framework will be used. The following assumptions will be made concerning juvenile court organization, its environment, and its associated practices:

1. The juvenile court operates with conflicting treatment and punishment functions and within a supporting environment characterized by uncertainty and scarcity of resources. This includes limited knowledge and operational technology on which to base youth treatment practices, shortages of personnel, limited budgetary allocations, and uncertainty regarding the number and nature of youths coming before the court.

2. Operational uncertainty predisposes the court to varieties of adaptations, programmatic modifications, and drift toward an opportunistic organizational character. Reform programs, operational changes, and internal decision-making steadily turn out to be consistent with the organization's self-interest in maintaining or enhancing its level of organization as well as with operating in an expeditious manner.

13

3. The court's organizational needs have been confused with the needs of youth. The maintenance and expansion requirements of the court organization and the court's subsequent adaptation to meet those needs have potentially the greatest impact on the determination of how youths will be handled. Court personnel commonly assume that programs and innovative service expansions within the court organization will result in more effective handling of youths. This idea is based on the notion that the court operates with ever-present budget and resource restrictions and constrained youth services.

4. The determination of which youths need a particular juvenile court service is largely a function of the available service alternatives. The choice of service alternatives fluctuates over time and across jurisdictions in relation to an individual court's response to various environmental pressures and opportunities. Service alternatives available to the juvenile court can include formal home supervision, foster home care, various local and state institutions, informal youth and family services, and so on. It is these service alternatives that provide the structural determinants of decision-making within the juvenile court. They constitute the system of action in which juvenile court personnel must operate, thereby limiting the range of possible court action in relation to problem youths.

To summarize: in this study, the juvenile court is viewed as a formal organization that operates with conflicting goals, limited technology, and financial instability. These conditions result in an operational uncertainty which lead the court to take on an opportunistic character that includes a readiness to incorporate a variety of reform programs such as community corrections. The nature of these programs shapes the court's capacity to respond to different groups of youths and/or family problems. The ever-present operational uncertainty also predisposes the court to implement reform programs that reinforce previous court practice instead of significantly restructuring them. The organizational context of the juvenile court influences the way the court implements reforms and subsequently handles youths. The nature of this organizational context of program alternatives, which confine and limit the court's possible

14

responses to youths and families, varies across jurisdictions and changes over time in relation to the juvenile court's initiative and response to various environmental opportunities and pressures.

OVERVIEW AND ORGANIZATION
OF BOOK

As stated earlier, this study has three central purposes. They are (1) to describe a juvenile court's experiences with three community correction reforms, (2) to document the net-widening effect resulting from the court's implementation of these reforms, and (3) to consider implications for future policy and evaluation that can be derived from the various unintended and intended results produced by community correction reforms. This threefold focus assumes that while all correction reform efforts are subject to drift during implementation, it is possible and necessary to evaluate the process to determine the results produced by a program's implementation. Findings from such evaluations will make it possible to specify what various reform programs which have been implemented can and cannot do and who they can and cannot affect.

The book is divided into seven chapters. Chapter 2 provides historical background on California's development of juvenile courts. Chapters 3, 4, and 5 present findings on the development, implementation, and system impact of three community correction reforms in a California juvenile court. Chapter 6 assesses the interrelation of juvenile court organizations, court reforms, and the net-widening phenomenon. The concluding chapter reviews diversion's mixed results reported nationwide and develops a multi-goal evaluation approach capable of differentiating what various correction reform programs can and cannot do for various youths given relatively stable program contexts.

NOTES

1. Rothman, D.J. The Discovery of the Asylum. Little, Brown and Company, 1971, pp. 1-78.

2. Rothman, D.J. The Discovery of the Asylum. Little, Brown and Company, 1971, pp. 70-108.

3. Hylton, J. Reintegrating the Offender: Assessing the Impact of Community Corrections. University Press of America, 1981, pp. 1-5.

4. Klein, M.W. "Deinstitutionalization and Diversion of Juvenile Offenders: A Litany of Impediments." In N. Morris and M. Tonry (eds.) Crime and Justice. University of Chicago Press, 1979, pp. 157-158.

5. Boole, K. L. The Juvenile Court: Its Origins, History and Procedure. Berkeley: University of California, 1928 Unpublished Doctoral Dissertation; Chute, C. "Fifty Years of the Juvenile Court." In National Probation and Parole Association Year Book, 1949, pp. 1-20; Dobbs, H. A. "In Defense of Juvenile Courts." In Federal Probation 13 (1949):24-29; Garabedian, P. G. and D. C. Gibbons. Becoming Delinquent: Young Offenders and the Correctional System. Aldine Publishing Company, 1970; Lou, H. H. Juvenile Courts in the United States. University of North Carolina Press, 1927; Teeters, N. K. and J. O. Reinneman. The Challenge of Delinquency. Prentice-Hall, Inc., 1950.

6. Allen, F. A. The Borderland of Criminal Justice: Essays in Criminology. University of Chicago Press, 1964; Arnold, M., "Juvenile Justice in Transition." UCLA Law Review 14 (1957):1144-1158; Caldwell, R. G. "The Juvenile Court: Its Development and Some Major Problems." Journal of Criminal Law, Criminology and Police Science 51 (1961):493-511; Handler, J. F. "The Juvenile Court and the Adversary System: Problems of Function and Form." Wisconsin Law Review (1965):7-51; Newman, G. G. (ed.) Children in the Courts: The Question of Representation. Institute of Continuing Legal Education, 1967; Rosenheim, M. Justice for the Child: A Juvenile Court in Transition. The Free Press of Glencoe, 1962, pp. 69-74; Tappan, P. W. Delinquent Girls in Court. Columbia University Press, 1947.

7. Tappan, p. 22.

8. Ward, R. H. "The Labeling Theory: A Critical Analysis." Criminology: An Interdisciplinary Journal 9 (1971):281.

16

9. Cicourel, A. The Social Organization of Juvenile Justice. John Wiley and Sons, Inc., 1968; Goldman, N. "The Differential Selection of Juvenile Offenders for Court Appearances." In W. Chambliss (ed.), Crime and the Legal Process. McGraw-Hill Book Company, 1969; Piliavin, I. and S. Briar. "Police Encounters with Juveniles." American Journal of Sociology 70 (1964):206-214; Thornberry, T. "Race, Socioeconomic Status and Sentencing in the Juvenile Justice System." Journal of Criminal Law and Criminology 64 (1973):90-98.

10. Hagan, J. "Extra-Legal Attributes and Criminal Sentencing: An Assessment of a Sociological Viewpoint." Law and Society Review 8 (1974):357-385; Ward, pp. 285-288; Wellford, C. "Labeling Theory and Criminology: An Assessment." Social Problems 22 (1975):332-345.

11. Black, D. and A. Reiss. "Police Control of Juveniles." American Sociological Review 37 (1970):63-77; Ferdinand, T. and E. Luchterhand "Inner City Youth, the Police, the Juvenile Court and Justice." Social Problems 18 (1962):510-527; Terry, R. "Discrimination in the Handling of Juvenile Offenders by Social Control Agencies." Journal of Research in Crime and Delinquency 4 (1967):218-230; Thomas, C. and C. Sieverdes. "Juvenile Court Intake: An Analysis of Discretional Decision-Making." Criminology 12 (1975):413-432; Wellford, pp. 332-345; Williams, J. and M. Gold. "From Delinquent Behaviors to Official Delinquency." Social Problems 20 (1972):209-227.

12. Cicourel, 1968; Emerson, R. M. Judging Delinquents Context and Process in Juvenile Court. Aldine Publishing Company, 1969.

13. Cicourel, pp. 168-169.

14. Emerson, p. 8.

15. The institutional school is best represented in the writings of Philip Selznick. See his "Foundations of a Theory of Organization." American Sociological Review 13 (1948):25-35; TVA and the Grass Roots. Harper Row, Inc., 1966; and Leadership in Administration. Row Peterson, 1957.

16. Perrow, C. Complex Organizations: A Critical Essay. Scott, Foresman and Company, 1972, pp. 178-204.

17. Perrow, p. 178.

18. Clark, B. The Open Door College: A Case Study. McGraw-Hill Book Company, 1960; Gusfield, J. Symbolic Crusade: Status Politics and the American Temperance Movement. University of Illinois Press, 1963; Messinger, S. L. "Organizational Transformation: A Case Study of a Declining Social Movement."

American Sociological Review 20 (1955):3-10; Sudnow, D. "The Public Defender." In R. D. Swartz and J. Skolnick (eds.), Society and the Legal Order. Basic Books, Inc., 1970.

19. Sudnow, p. 392.

20. For example, see Cressey, D. R. "Achievement of an Unstated Organizational Goal: An Observation of Prisons." Pacific Sociological Review 1 (1958):43-49; Street, D., R. Vinter and C. Perrow. Organizations for Treatment. The Free Press, 1966; Zald, M. N. "The Correctional Institution for Juvenile Offenders: An Analysis of Organizational 'Character'." Social Problems 8 (1960):57-67.

21. Perrow, Complex Organizations, pp. 187-188.

22. Selznick, Leadership in Administration, pp. 5-22.

23. For a critical discussion of the organizational-institutional distinction, see Wolin, S. S. "A Critique of Organizational Theories." In A. Etzioni (ed.), A Sociological Reader in Complex Organizations, 2nd ed. Holt, Rinehart and Winston, Inc., 1969, pp. 133-149.

24. Perrow, Complex Organizations, p. 199.

25. Perrow, Complex Organizations, pp. 199-204.

26. Gore, W. J. Administrative Decision-Making: A Heuristic Model. John Wiley and Sons, Inc., 1964, p. 22.

27. Cole, G. F. Politics and the Administration of Justice. Sage Publications, 1973, p. 58.

28. Levine, S. and P. White. "Exchange as a Conceptual Framework for the Study of Interorganizational Relationships." In A. Etzioni (eds.), A Sociological Reader on Complex Organizations, 2nd ed. Holt, Rinehart and Winston, Inc., 1969, p. 131.

29. The California Youth Authority administers the state youth reformatories and parole services which the county juvenile courts use for placement of their most serious youth cases.

30. Levine and White, p. 121.

31. Cole, p. 62.

32. The Juvenile Justice Commission is an eight member citizen board that is responsible for the supervision and annual assessments of county juvenile court practices.

33. Cole, p. 63.

34. Thompson, J. D. and W. J. McEwen. "Organizational Goals and Environment." In A. Etzioni (ed.), A Sociological Reader on Complex Organizations, 2nd ed. Holt, Rinehart and Winston, Inc., 1969, p. 193.

35. For discussion, see Feeley, M. "Two Models of the Criminal Justice System: An Organizational Perspective." Law and Society Review 7 (1973):407-425.

36. Feeley, p. 414.

37. For discussion, see Skolnick, J. "The Sociology of Law in America." Law and Society Summer Supplement (1969):15-18.

CHAPTER 2

HISTORY OF CALIFORNIA JUVENILE COURTS

Underlying this study's perspective on the juvenile court is the assumption that the court is characterized by ever-present conditions of operational uncertainty which contribute to its opportunistic character. This study contends that because of this operational uncertainty and opportunism, the juvenile court responds to, implements, and shapes the impact of correction reform programs in ways aimed at reducing its own uncertainty rather than in ways consistent with the conceptual rationales that underly the reforms.

This chapter describes how the court's organizational character has evolved. Its primary purpose is to demonstrate how the court's early development has contributed to its opportunistic character.

PRE-JUVENILE COURT ERA

As previously stated, institutionalization became a means of handling deviant youths in the early nineteenth century, coinciding with that period's belief that society could not maintain social order without organized reform. The basic premise was that crime did not reflect an inherent depravity in children but was the consequence of a socially disorganized society.

Belief in the perfectability of youths and the societal causes of crime led to development of the youth reformatory. The underlying idea of reformatories, as well as adult prisons, was that an uncorrupted environment would provide youths and adults the moral and physical abilities they needed to combat the dangers that were rampant in nineteenth century America. As Rothman states,

> The promise of institutionalization depended upon the isolation of the prisoner and the establishment of a disciplined routine. Convinced that deviancy was primarily the result of the corruptions prevading the community, and that organizations like the family and the church were not counterbalancing them, they believed that a setting which removed the offender from all temptations and substituted a steady and regular regimen would reform him. Since the convict was not inherently depraved, but the victim of an upbringing that had failed to

20

provide protection against the vices at loose in society, a well-ordered institution could successfully reeducate and rehabilitate him. The penitentiary, free of corruption and dedicated to the proper training of the inmate, would inculcate the discipline that negligent parents, evil companions, taverns, houses of prostitution, theaters, and gambling halls had destroyed. Just as the criminal's environment had led him into crime, the institutional environment would lead him out of it.[1]

The two central functions of the youth reformatory were (1) to provide shelter from an "improper" environment and (2) to rehabilitate, reform, or change young deviants into law-abiding citizens. Like the mental hospital and the penitentiary, the reformatory was to change people through a program emphasizing order, routine, discipline, and strict obedience. As Platt states,

> The reformatory system was based on the assumption that proper training can counteract the impositions of poor family life, a corrupt environment, and poverty, while at the same time toughening and preparing delinquents for the struggle ahead.[2]

Correction reformers assumed that deviants were susceptible to change. Youth offenders were thought to be especially susceptible, since they were not as "fixed" in deviant lifestyles as adult offenders.

Between 1825 and 1830, New York, Boston, and Philadelphia established houses of refuge. However, separate facilities for delinquent youths were slow to develop. Many urban centers used orphanages as multifunction institutions. But between 1840 and 1857, specialization had increased and seventeen reformatories were operating with a combined inmate population of more than twenty thousand.[3]

The 1850s were a significant period in the development of juvenile reformatories, primarily because of the growing disillusionment with penitentiaries cited earlier. During this decade it became evident that prisons were not fulfilling their promise of rehabilitation. This resulted in a renewed interest in differentiating between juvenile and adult offenders. At the turn of the century, juvenile courts were becoming prevalent across the United States as a means to differentiate further between youthful offenders and adult offenders in order to increase the success of rehabilitation.

21

CALIFORNIA'S DEVELOPMENT
OF JUVENILE COURTS

Juvenile Court Law

The first juvenile court was created in Cook County, Illinois in 1899. California enacted a juvenile court law in 1903 after strong lobbying by several women's groups. These groups argued that children's cases were being heard with and in a manner similar to adult cases. This assertion is substantiated partially by records of state reform school commitments. For example, of the total number of boys committed to California's Preston School of Industry before 1900, 70 percent were committed by the superior court (i.e., the criminal court) and the remaining 30 percent by police, justices, and recorders' courts.[4] However, most youthful offenders never reached the state reformatory level. In these instances, treatment was provided through informal arrangements with the police, family, or local community.[5]

The issue of differential treatment before the inception of the juvenile court is not of particular significance here. However, it should be recognized that long before juvenile courts existed, youths were not, as a rule, incarcerated with adults, harsh sentences for trivial offenses were the exceptions, and capital punishment for a juvenile offender was almost unknown. Furthermore, recent studies have suggested that saving children was not the only concern of those who argued for the foundation of juvenile courts. These studies contend that the "child savers" were interested also in imposing white middle-class standards on urban youths of minority or immigrant backgrounds. Therefore, in addition to criminal acts, juvenile court jurisdiction included such offenses as truancy, disobedience to parents, and being "in danger of living an idle, lewd, or immoral life."[6]

Nonetheless, before the development of the juvenile court, youths involved in more serious offenses were being arrested and jailed with adults. Of particular concern to the reformers, as Lemert points out, were

> the visible aspects of juvenile justice--namely, public arrests, transportation to jail in paddy wagons, open hearings in court along with criminals, misdemeanants, and prostitutes.[7]

These "visible aspects" provided the reformers with illustrations to emphasize in their lobbying efforts. Yet despite impressive preparation, organization, and a state-wide campaign, the 1903 California Act was secured only after a compromise agreement that public funds would not be used to pay the salaries of the court's probation officers.

The 1903 Act provided for state control, protection, and treatment of dependent as well as delinquent children less than sixteen years old. Counties with more than one superior court judge were required to designate one or more judges whose particular task it was to hear in special session cases coming under juvenile court jurisdiction. There were three other major provisions of the 1903 Act:8

1. No court could commit a child under twelve to a jail, prison, or police station. However, if such a child were unable to furnish bail, he could be committed to the care of the sheriff, police officer, constable, or probation officer.

2. The superior court of each county could appoint a board of six citizens to serve the county without compensation. Their duties would be the investigation of all societies, associations, and corporations receiving children under this act.

3. Any judge of superior court should have the authority to appoint or designate one or more persons to act as probation officers and to serve at the pleasure of the court.

Because probation officers' salaries could not be drawn from public funds, private sources were sought. In San Francisco County, for example, The Boys' and Girls' Aid Society, The California Club, and Associated Charities provided the officers' salaries.9

In 1905, responding to recommendations by the Board of Charities and Corrections (predecessor to the State Department of Welfare), the legislature amended the 1903 Act in several respects. The investigating board of six citizens was replaced by a seven-member probation committee. Committee members were to be appointed by the county's superior court judges. Probation officers were to be appointed for two-year terms by the probation committee of each county and, significantly, their salaries were to come from county treasuries.10

The next major development in California's juvenile court movement occurred following the 1908 conference of the State Board of Charities and Corrections. The conference was attended by superior court judges, district attorneys, county probation committee members, probation officers, and officials from the

Whittier State and Preston School reformatories. The purpose of the conference was to discuss general problems with the existing juvenile court legislation and to draw up recommendations to be presented to the state legislature. The following recommendations were adopted at the conference: [11]

1. That the Probation Committee should be retained and that the power to nominate the probation officers is not unconstitutional and should be retained.

2. That, in the larger counties, the law make it mandatory upon the Board of Supervisors to provide a detention home.

3. That probation officers should be paid a salary from the county treasury.

4. That a parental or adult contributory delinquency and dependency law is necessary.

5. That the age of majority for girls be raised from eighteen to twenty-one years.

6. That the ages for commitment to both Whittier State and Preston School of Industry be fixed at between nine and nineteen.

7. That the laws governing the two reform schools be withdrawn so as to make them conform with respect to commitments, with the exception that girls be committed to Whittier only and the Preston School provide for the commitment of dependent male children.

8. That commitments to Whittier and Preston schools are to be considered rather in the nature of guardianship than as punishment for crimes, and these institutions as schools and not prisons. In such cases, a trial by jury is not essential.

In 1909, the legislature responded to these recommendations with another juvenile court law. The new legislation embodied most of the 1908 conference recommendations. Its major features were the following:

1. The creation of a special court to deal with children

2. The requirement of a probation committee in each county

3. The placement of children on probation instead of in prison

4. The provision of a paid probation officer or officers for each county

5. The severing of parents' rights to child custody in cases where the welfare of the child required it

6. The extension of juvenile court jurisdiction to adults found to be contributing to the delinquency of a minor and making such offense a misdemeanor

The 1909 legislation defined a delinquent youth as any person under eighteen years old who was found to have violated any law of the State or any ordinance of a town, city, or county.

A dependent child was defined as a person under eighteen who was found to be

> begging or receiving alms; in streets or public places; a vagrant; wandering without a home or means of subsistence; without parent or guardian or without proper control; destitute; with an unfit home; in the company of criminals or prostitutes; living or being in a house of prostitution; habitually frequenting places where liquors are sold; refusing to obey reasonable parental orders or incorrigible; without proper parents; habitually truant; or habitually using intoxicating liquors.[12]

In 1911 the juvenile court law was modified to include jurisdiction over all youth under twenty-one. Probation officers were to be nominated by county probation committees and appointed by the judges. However, by 1914 many local judges and probation officers considered the existing law unworkable. That year the Board of Charities and Corrections met and acknowledged that there was general dissatisfaction in the counties with the present juvenile court law. Lemert suggests that during this period there was conflict between moral-reform groups and juvenile court

25

officials.[13] Judges and probation officers did not want to be restricted by legal directives in handling children or removing them from parental custody. One judge of this period commented:

> I sincerely trust no attempt will be made to prescribe the exact processes that the court should follow in these cases. The legislature should lay down the essentials which are to govern. That ground has generally been covered. Beyond that, the legislature should not circumscribe the exercise of judicial authority in these cases.[14]

In 1915 the state legislature repealed all past juvenile court legislation and passed a comprehensive juvenile court statute that prevailed until 1961. The new statute maintained juvenile court wardship over youths younger than twenty-one adjudged on the basis of the "dependent" criteria articulated in the 1909 legislation. However, the 1915 statute did not provide distinctions between delinquent, dependent, and neglected children.

California's Quest for Uniformity in Juvenile Court Practice

Of particular significance were the wide jurisdiction and multiple functions generated by statute without specific directives to guide the counties in implementing juvenile court law. This ambiguous legislation resulted ultimately in the "divergent evolution"[15] of juvenile court practices. The divergent evolution was exemplified by the different forms and uses of probation, detention, and probation committees across counties during the early years of juvenile court implementation.

In an attempt to check the divergent evolution, the state provided counties technical consultive services consistent with state law. The approach was initiated by the Board of Charities and Corrections and continued by its successors, the Department of Welfare and the Youth Authority. No attempt was made to gain county juvenile court compliance through legal intervention before 1961. The activities of the State Board of Charities and Corrections and the Department of Welfare were based on the conviction that the state's technical consultation would provide communication that would lead to common agreement and consensus between state and counties. Lemert writes:

> Both the Board of Charities and Corrections and its successor, the Department of Welfare, leaned heavily on individual contacts, and

26

local and state conferences and institutes,
in their search for a common foundation of
practice among those administering the
juvenile court law. Behind these methods lay
a conviction that discussion would lead to a
working consensus, which would cause judges
and probation officers to modify day to day
operation in line with objectives outlined in
the law.[16]

The Youth Authority, established in the 1940s, had, but never
exercised, formal authority over annual county court reports and
local detention and probation practices. Instead it relied on a
service approach, as had its predecessors.

The State Board of Charities and Corrections, for example, in
its first attempt to assess juvenile court practices by gathering
statistics for county comparisons had found the necessary
statistics were either inadequate or nonexistent.[17] But it did
find wide variations in probation committee activities and noted
the absence of legislatively mandated probation committees in ten
counties. Further variations were evident in county uses of
detention. In response to these variations, the board instituted
the newsletter Probation Letters to provide a medium for informing
probation officers about the court activities of other counties.

The one instance, for example, when the board compiled
information about county detention practices, it found and
reported that fifty-four counties detained juveniles in some way.
Forms of detention included boarding homes (twenty-two counties),
specially designed detention homes (sixteen counties), county
hospitals (nine counties), and subsidized homes (six counties).
One county shared the detention home run by an adjoining county.[18]
The board subsequently made a more comprehensive study of nine
counties to determine whether detention homes were necessary and,
if so, what their functions should be. On the basis of this
survey, the board adopted a series of detention home practices.

The Department of Welfare assumed responsibility for juvenile
court services in 1929. They took an approach to change similar
to that of the State Board of Charities and Corrections, also
expecting to accomplish local compliance with state laws and
recommended standards through communication. The Department of
Welfare continued to organize local and statewide conferences for
discussion of problems in court services and practices, and to
search for solutions mutually acceptable to state and county. The
Probation News, a monthly journal, was first published during this
period to provide miscellaneous news for probation officers.
Lemert describes the content and significance of this publication:

27

Communication with probation officers was further amplified through the monthly publication of Probation News. This proved to be little more than a bulletin whose news items and comments were pervaded by the values and ideology espoused in the rising field of social work. At the same time, the News struck a much more legalistic note than was true in the older Charities and Corrections Board reports. The attention of probation officers was regularly directed to appellate court decisions and Attorney General opinions bearing on the juvenile court and occasionally the items took sharp, didactic form, more or less instructing workers on procedures required by law.19

Several dominant concerns about court service during this period were the needs for separate detention facilities for youths, a prohibition on detention without court order, closed hearings for youths, and reports to be submitted by county probation committees to the state on an annual basis.

The Department of Welfare did not take legal action against counties that did not comply with juvenile court law despite the fact that some were occasionally in blatant violation of that law.

In the middle 1930s an attempt was made to initiate a state system of probation to overcome the disparities in juvenile court practices. Ultimately the proposal was discarded because of county-state jurisdictional disputes. Smaller counties were not at all amenable to a plan that would diminish their sovereignty. Their opposition prevented state legislation, and as a result, juvenile court practices continued to be essentially determined by the counties.20

California's attempts to standardize juvenile court practices decreased with the depression years and the United States' entry into World War II. It has been suggested by several writers that during this time the U.S. began its move toward an administrative state. Indicators included the takeover of many local welfare services by federal and state governments accompanied by sweeping economic changes.21

California's development of the California Youth Authority in 1941 was an example of the centralized administrative trend in government. The enabling legislation, The Youth Correction Authority Act, was patterned after the American Law Institutes' (ALI) Model Youth Correction Authority Act. Smith claims that while "coming closer than any subsequent Youth Authority Act in other states, the California legislation did not achieve the model structure envisioned by ALI," [22] and points out that both the Model Act and the California Act were "natural responses to the social demands being exerted in 1940 and 1941, urging that something be done about justice for youth." [23]

In compliance with the 1941 legislation, the governor appointed a three-person commission (The Youth Authority) whose primary duty was to submit state-committed youths (ages sixteen to twenty-three) to diagnostic examination in order to determine their treatment needs and to provide for the treatment. The type of treatment could vary from institutionalization to release under supervision. Section 1700 of the California Welfare and Institutions Code specified that the Youth Authority was to be a more effective protector of society by replacing retributive punishment with training and treatment directed toward the correction and rehabilitation of youthful offenders. In effect, California's establishment of the Youth Authority was a move toward centralized administration of justice to youths.

Shortly after the establishment of the Youth Authority, there were two suicides and a number of runaway incidents at the Whittier State School, an institution that had also gone through seven different superintendents in a single year. Furthermore, there were periodic difficulties with the other two state youth correction schools. [24] Public concern and pressure over these incidents--concern which included an Assembly Interim Committee investigation--led Governor Earl Warren to request that the newly established Youth Authority assume management of the state's three youth reformatories and its parole services. In 1943 the legislature confirmed the Youth Authority's responsibility for these institutions and for parole functions. Subsequent amendments assigned the Youth Authority limited duties and control in connection with juvenile court standards. Some of these duties included setting detention and probation standards, inspecting juvenile halls (detention facilities and county camps receiving state subsidy), and requiring annual probation reports from counties. The penalties for nonconforming counties were never specified, and the Youth Authority never asserted formal authority over counties for noncompliance.

The Youth Authority, like the State Board of Charities and Corrections and Department of Welfare before it, relied on conferences and statewide committee meetings to achieve county uniformity in juvenile court practices. Typically, recommendations that arose from these conferences were compiled and distributed to each county. Smith cites a particular problem between the Youth Authority and counties that was resolved by a conference. In 1955, county juvenile court judges and Youth Authority officials were brought together to discuss the excessive county detention (one to six months) of youths awaiting state reformatory placement. Subsequently many judges began to grant

29

probation in cases that previously would have resulted in a state reformatory commitment. Shortly thereafter, the Youth Authority found its reformatories with empty beds and had to modify the policy agreed upon.[25]

Beyond the use of conferences and committees, the Youth Authority's Field Services Division conducted initial surveys on a wide range of county activities pertaining to youths including law enforcement, schools, recreation, traffic courts, juvenile court, and probation.[26] Generally the counties brought in Youth Authority consultants to help them deal with their court service-related problems. According to the probation officer of the juvenile court under study (hereafter referred to as North County),

> the Youth Authority's Field Services used the
> consultant service method. They assisted us
> with our problems, they were not an
> edict-issuing agency, they did not try to
> shove practices down our throats.[27]

The probation officer cited North County's decision to construct a larger detention facility in the late 1940s. The county questioned what sort of services should be included in a detention facility. A Youth Authority detention consultant was called in and recommended to the county that, in addition to a lock-up facility, the detention center should include school, counseling, and medical and psychological diagnostic services. In this way, the Youth Authority not only provided a needed service to the county but was able to recommend its standards in an unofficial manner.

Overall, the Youth Authority's role in influencing juvenile court practices, though its approach was similar to that of the two previous state agencies, was an improvement over the role played by its predecessors because of its greater staff and financial resources. Most of the Youth Authority's staff were drawn from either Los Angeles or Alameda Counties. Given that and the unclear juvenile court legislation, it is not surprising that the juvenile court standards developed by the Youth Authority reflected practices in those counties.[28] Furthermore, most Youth Authority personnel had social work backgrounds which influenced their recommendations to local courts for casework techniques in probation practice.

A retired Youth Authority consultant stated in an interview that the Youth Authority took a gradual, one-step-at-a-time approach in its attempt to secure consensus in juvenile court practices. "We were realistic and recognized the reluctance of the counties to be dictated to by the state. Therefore, we relied on the setting example and persuasion approach."[29] The Youth

Authority recognized that local probation officers came from diverse backgrounds (law enforcement, business, religion, etc.) and that uniformity of practice could not be expected without developing a series of county contacts and relying on county "experiences." The Youth Authority consultants felt that as the counties experienced normal operating difficulties they would, with Youth Authority assistance, reach consensus on "appropriate" court services and practices.

In addition to the Youth Authority's belief in eventual county-state consensus through experience, the strong sense of "localism" (self-determination) in state politics was not taken lightly. The State Senate had strong rural representation, and "home rule" was felt to be a right of local government. As the Youth Authority consultant points out:

> The people of Humbolt County did not want Los Angeles County Court practices rammed down their throats. Los Angeles' needs and problems with youths were not the same as Humbolt County's.[30]

The Youth Authority attempted to deal with the strong "localism" sentiment through a gradual step-by-step "upgrading" process. Both Youth Authority Director Karl Holton and especially his successor, Heman Stark, believed that in time the counties would share the state's ideas about court services and practices. Stark's successful public relations approach with the Probation Officers Association is widely acknowledged. He established strong working relationships with the probation leaders across the state. Many probation officers, far from thinking that Stark was seeking state control over court functions, thought his motives were good. This perception contributed toward more ready acceptance by court authorities of state-sponsored court programs.[31]

As cited previously, during the late 1940s and early 1950s, the Youth Authority studied court services in individual counties. These studies were broad surveys concerned primarily with law enforcement and probation problems. Stark used the surveys to further the Youth Authority's attempt to reach uniformity in court services and to gain credibility with counties as a "service" agency oriented toward local assistance rather than control. For example, the process of developing a detention facility in North County began with a meeting of the probation officer, Stark, and Youth Authority consultants to discuss problems and to work out any areas of disagreement. Following the meeting, the Youth Authority helped the probation officer bargain with local interest groups and the Board of Supervisors to gain approval for the allocation of funds for the detention facility.

Another major method the Youth Authority used to gain compliance in court practices was state subsidization of court services. State subsidy programs were first considered by the Department of Welfare in the 1930s, but the Department could not overcome strong "localism" sentiments or the fear of ultimate state control, so no subsidy program materialized. Counties were not interested in programs that carried the possibility of any state interference in county government. Like federal grants-in-aid, state subsidy was directed toward initiating the development of specific services. The first Youth Authority subsidy was made available in 1945 in a program to encourage counties to develop local institutions for problem youths as alternatives to state reformatories. Counties that received subsidies were subject to subsequent Youth Authority regulation of the standards of the local youth institution.

In summary: changes in California's juvenile court law from 1903 to 1961 can be described as halting steps toward achieving uniformity in local policy and legalizing practices already in effect. This pattern of reactive legislation amounted to state approval of county solutions to local problems. However, the juvenile court legislation was responsive primarily to the problems of the larger counties--namely, Los Angeles, San Francisco, and Alameda. Because of this urban bias, the smaller counties tended to resist the law or interpret it in a way that met their own needs.

Eventually, the Youth Authority realized that consultant services, statewide conferences, and distribution of probation publications were not sufficient to move juvenile court service and practice in particular directions. Consequently, it undertook the subsidy approach which to date has had the greatest impact of any of the state's attempts to influence juvenile court services and practices.

Until the 1950s, juvenile courts in California had, in effect, developed largely without clear legal directives or sufficient knowledge and financial bases. These conditions contributed to operational uncertainty and the consequent opportunistic character of the juvenile court organization which supported a resistance in the court to state sponsored court services and practices that were not accompanied by substantial state funding.

HISTORICAL BACKGROUND OF NORTH
COUNTY'S JUVENILE COURT

In 1909 a prominent local industrialist was appointed as North County's first probation officer. The probation officer was to serve the juvenile court part-time and handle both child and adult cases that were granted probation by the courts. From 1909 to 1927 North County's juvenile court services consisted of a juvenile court judge, a part-time probation officer, and a part-time detention facility located in the county hospital's mental ward. Delinquents and dependents were not separated except in instances of overcrowding, when delinquents were held in the county jail.

In 1927 North County appointed a local minister as its first full-time probation officer and constructed a small detention facility on the county hospital grounds to house twelve dependent, neglected, or delinquent youths. However, most delinquent youths were held in the county jail because the increasing number of youths detained by the county exceeded the low capacity of the detention home. In 1939 a female probation assistant was appointed on a part-time basis to handle girls' and women's cases.

The juvenile court judge who served in North County from 1936 to 1946 suggested in interviews that before the late 1930s the county classified problem children into two categories. "A child was either 'bad' enough to go to a state reformatory or 'good' enough to remain at home."[32] This resulted in two types of court disposition--state reformatory commitment or home probation supervision.

In the late 1930s and the subsequent war years, North County's probation personnel and detention facility were substantially overburdened. In 1940 the probation staff was the same as it had been in 1927. The juvenile court judge reflected that during this era the county was inundated by a rural southern population that migrated to North County for employment in the shipyards. The population of the county's major city jumped from 25,000 in 1941 to more than 100,000 by 1943. The judge elaborated; there was

> a considerable lack of morality, a great deal
> of incest between fathers and daughters,
> stealing was common practice despite the
> higher than usual shipyard salaries, and
> truancy was rampant.[33]

Many of the county schools were on a four-shift schedule, and the judge reasoned youths had nothing else to do but get into trouble.

In response to the rising number of youths in trouble and their presumed bad homes, the county abandoned its previous reliance on the two-category disposition system. Private institutions and foster home placements were developed and used frequently by the court. The private institutions, with the exception of the Salvation Army Boys' and Girls' Home, were youth homes sponsored by the Catholic Church. Because of a lag in state reformatory construction, the Youth Authority was not a major placement resource for the county during this period.

After the war the county expected a significant decrease in youths requiring court services, but it did not materialize. In fact, the number of juvenile court orders increased from 801 in 1945 to 1,109 in 1946. The county assumed that the number of youths requiring court services would continue to increase, and as a result, expansion of court services was recommended. The following excerpt from the County's 1946 Annual Probation Report reflects the thinking:

> It was supposed by many that there would be a great falling off in juvenile delinquency in the county. Judging from what has happened during the first two months of the current year, it would seem that the juvenile problem is definitely and steadily becoming greater.[34]

The report went on to argue for expansion of court services including a new detention facility or juvenile hall and additional probation staff and psychiatric services.

The North County probation officer who assumed the position in 1945 claimed that the first major development in the county's juvenile court services occurred with the construction of a new juvenile hall. Development of the hall won the Board of Supervisor's approval only after the juvenile court judge bargained with a property owner and was able to secure the needed land at two-thirds its market value. As previously mentioned, a Youth Authority consultant assisted the county in planning the juvenile hall services. This is reflected in the following acknowledgment by the county in its 1950 Annual Probation Report:

> A close working relationship has been continued between the Superintendent of the Juvenile Hall and the Detention Consultant for the California Youth Authority. The Consultant assisted in a statistical survey of the length of periods of detention for delinquent and neglected children. The Juvenile Hall Superintendent was affiliated with a group of near-by juvenile hall superintendents who met monthly with the Youth Authority Consultant. These sessions and visits to other juvenile halls offered opportunities for the exchange of ideas on various phases of juvenile hall work.[35]

34

The hall also included custodial facilities, school, counseling, medical, and psychiatric diagnostic services. Construction was completed in 1949, and the hall began operation in 1950.

Between 1950 and 1951 the court's probation caseloads increased 15.4 percent, new juvenile referrals rose from 1,324 to 1,890, and juvenile hall admissions jumped from 1,110 to 1,526. Of particular significance was that 50 percent of the youths detained at juvenile hall were awaiting state reformatory placements and spent an average of three months there before that placement. In response to this particular detention problem, the court began to campaign for a local correction institution to reduce the court's reliance on state institutions. The following chapter will assess North County's experiences with a local youth institution.

Overall, between 1909 and 1950, juvenile court services and related court practices in North County as in other California counties, developed as local accommodations in response to perceived local needs. Juvenile court law and the various state agencies played a limited role in determining local court services or practices. Without benefit of consistent goals, lacking sufficient operational technology, and embedded in local environments characterized by financial scarcity, juvenile court organizations became characterized by operational uncertainty and opportunism. The next three chapters consider how the court's opportunistic character influenced North County's experiences with a series of community correction reforms.

NOTES

1.   Rothman, D. J. The Discovery of the Asylum. Little, Brown and Company, 1971, pp. 82-83.

2.   Platt, A. M. The Child Savers. The University of Chicago Press, 1969.

3.   Rothman, p. 209.

4.   Preston School of Industry, Fourth Biennial Report of the Board of Trustees, 1898-1900, p. 17.

5.   For discussion of the differential handling of youthful offenders before juvenile courts see Platt, pp. 183-202.

6.   Platt, pp. 137-145.

7.   Lemert, E. M. Social Action and Legal Change: Revolution Within the Juvenile Court. Aldine Publishing Company, 1970.

8.   Cahn, F. and V. Bary. Welfare Activities of Federal, State and Local Governments in California 1850-1934. University of California Press, 1936.

9.   Cahn and Bary, p. 73.

10.   Cahn and Bary, p. 73.

11.   Cahn and Bary, p. 74.

12.   Cahn and Bary, p. 73.

13.   Lemert, p. 23 and p. 40.

14.   Transactions of the Commonwealth Club of California, Vol. V. San Francisco, 1910, p. 248.

15.   Lemert, pp. 41-46.

16.   Lemert, p. 47.

17   Cahn and Bary, p. 78.

18.   Cahn and Bary, p. 81.

19.   Lemert, pp. 47-48.

20.   Lemert, p. 49.

21. Lemert, p. 49.

22. Smith, R. L. Youth and Correction: An Institutional Analysis of the California Youth Authority. Berkeley: University of California, 1955 Unpublished Master's Thesis, p. 6.

23. Smith, p. 6.

24. Underwood, W. Unpublished historical account of the California Youth Authority. California Department of the Youth Authority, 1968.

25. Smith, p. 64.

26. Lemert, p. 57.

27. Interview with North County probation officer.

28. Interview with a California Youth Authority consultant under directors Karl Holton, Heman Stark, and Allan Breed.

29. Interview with a California Youth Authority consultant.

30. Interview with a California Youth Authority consultant.

31. Interview with a California Youth Authority consultant.

32. Interview with North County's previous juvenile court judge who served from 1936 to 1946.

33. Interview with North County's previous juvenile court judge who served from 1936 to 1946.

34. North County Annual Probation Report, 1946.

35. North County Annual Probation Report, 1950.

CHAPTER 3

BOYS' CENTER

This assessment of North County juvenile court's experience with three community correction reforms will give equal consideration to the developmental background, the implementation, and the system impact of each reform (see Appendix for discussion of the research methods of this study). The purpose of this triple focus is to demonstrate the interrelation in the court organization among these three elements--how and why the court responds to, implements, and ultimately shapes the impact of reform programs.

This chapter assesses the Boys' Treatment Center (hereafter called Boys' Center), a local institution officially aimed at providing an alternative to state reformatories. The assessment documents the proposition that the Boys' Center was promoted by the court as a mechanism that would respond to and fulfill the multiple needs and requirements of special interests groups--court organization, youth treatment, and the state. When it was implemented, the Boys' Center's program reflected an attempt to reach multiple goals, thereby serving a variety of troubled youths. The result was that the Boys' Center emerged not as an alternative to state reformatories but as an institutional supplement. This had a net-widening effect, by which a larger proportion of the court's boys' cases became subject to institutional control.

DEVELOPMENTAL BACKGROUND OF BOYS' CENTER

The California Youth Authority was established in 1941. Within ten years, the state's total population increased 50 percent. During this same period, the state's youth reformatory population almost doubled, from 1,300 in 1941 to 2,526 in 1953. Historically the state's response to increased commitments had been to build more institutions. However, during World War II and the early 1950s there were lags in state reformatory construction while the number of court commitments to state reformatories continued to climb. The result by the early 1950s was long local detention waits (three to six months) for youths awaiting reformatory placement.

The increase in court commitments to state reformatories has been attributed to a conflict in the way the state and the courts thought about the appropriate use of state institutions. It has been argued that the juvenile courts believed Youth Authority reformatories provided greater treatment opportunities and more security than did local court programs.[1] However, Karl Holton, Youth Authority Director from 1941 until 1952, attributed frequent court commitment of youths to state reformatories to the judges' "erroneous attitudes."[2] His feelings, as well as those of Heman Stark (Youth Authority Director in 1952), were that state reformatories were the appropriate alternative only after all local efforts had failed.

In an attempt to solve this court-state problem, the Governor's Conference on Children and Youth was held in 1948, 1950, and 1954. These conferences, instigated by the Youth Authority, found that many children were being held in detention unnecessarily. For example, in 1952 a special study about court detention and child care conducted by the Governor's Children and Youth Committee determined that 41 percent of the state's entire detention population was being held without justification. The study concluded on the basis of national averages, California was detaining a higher percentage of its arrested youths than any other state.

In effect, in the absence of state reformatory openings or local institutional alternatives, courts began using their juvenile halls (detention facilities) for multiple functions.[3] This was demonstrated in a 1958 survey by the Governor's Juvenile Justice Commission, which concluded that 28 percent of California's probation officers believed detention to be therapeutically valuable. The survey also concluded that 40 percent of the juvenile court judges felt detention was justified to ensure a child's appearance in court.[4] Those who opposed the detention-treatment or the insurance-of-court-appearance rationales for detention argued that detention was not the time or the place for treatment and that citations would work just as well to ensure a child's appearance in court.[5]

The detention issue dates back to California's early juvenile court acts and amendments. Despite the persistence of this issue, clear detention guidelines for courts to follow were not formulated until 1960. The Youth Authority, true to its service tradition, had attempted to influence local detention practices by providing the courts with special detention consultants and arranging conferences where a number of juvenile hall superintendents met and exchanged ideas about detention. In addition, Holton and Stark had encouraged the statewide surveys to illustrate detention abuses and disparities.

The new Juvenile Hall in North County began operation in 1950. This facility increased the county's detention capacity from twenty-seven to eighty children. In the 1950 Annual Probation Report, the purpose and admission criteria of the hall were stated as follows:

39

Its function is to provide short term care for children who come under the jurisdiction of the Juvenile Court. These include delinquent and neglected children who cannot safely be left at home pending disposition of their cases by the Juvenile Court. Juvenile Hall is not a penal or correctional institution. In accordance with the law, as well as the policies and programs of the department, Juvenile Hall is operated as nearly as possible in a homelike fashion. A conscientious effort is made by the department to admit for detention or shelter only those children whose needs and problems require that they be in Juvenile Hall. [6]

In 1950 the Juvenile Hall admitted a total of 1,110 youths, compared to 927 in 1949, and 904 in 1948. In 1951, Juvenile Hall admissions jumped to 1,527 with an average daily population of 75, a 37.3 percent increase from the 1950 daily average. The court estimated that 25 to 50 percent of the youths were awaiting state reformatory placements, which resulted in three-month detention waits after court appearances. In response to the significant increase in the Juvenile Hall population, the juvenile court began to argue for a local "treatment" institution as an alternative to state reformatory commitments and their accompanying long waits in detention. The 1951 Annual Probation Report argued:

At the present time from twenty-five percent to fifty percent of the boys detained at the Juvenile Hall are waiting to be delivered to a State Training School. Each boy committed waits about three months in Juvenile Hall after his court appearance. If it were possible to move these boys out of Juvenile Hall immediately after commitment, the detention load would be considerably lightened. The best method of solving this problem is to provide a county operated training facility for boys where the majority of them could be sent immediately. [7]

From 1952 through 1956, the Juvenile Hall population and state reformatory commitments stabilized. Although the actual figures in the 1952-1956 period were higher than those in the late 1940s and early 1950s, the annual percentage increase had subsided (see Table 3.1 on next page). Nonetheless, by June of 1953, the juvenile court had successfully convinced local political interests and the Board of Supervisors of the need for a local institution.

Table 3.1

Juvenile Hall Admissions, Daily
Population, and State Reformatory Commitments [8]

Year	Yearly Admissions	Average Daily Population	Yearly State Reformatory Commitments
1944	789	21	
1945	932	25	32
1946	911	31	15
1947	849	40	21
1948	904	49	20
1949	927	50	30
1950	1,110	47	25
1951	1,527	75	22
1952	1,585	74	43
1953	1,799	76	63
1954	1,787	74	51
1955	1,653	75	80
1956	1,727	86	51

North County was concerned with reducing its detention load of boys when preliminary plans for the Boys' Center were initiated. The probation officer summarized:

> There was a major detention problem associated with the backlog of boys awaiting state reformatory placements. Furthermore, North County was growing fast and it was anticipated that this growth would continue.

To overcome both the immediate detention backlog and the projected increase of youth contacts, the court sought to expand itself through the development of the Boys' Center.

41

State Support for
Local Institutions

California's local correction institutions for youths began
in Los Angeles County in 1932. A Los Angeles County camp was
established by state subsidy to cope with transient youths who
were said to be coming to the Los Angeles area in great numbers
during the depression. In this period, Los Angeles' available
detention facilities were filled to maximum capacity, and
continuing arrivals made it necessary to return the boys to their
point of origin at county expense. Transients throughout the
nation learned: "If you ride the rods out to California, they
will send you home on the cushions."

Several amusing incidents illustrate the not-so-amusing
problem. One small boy promised the judge to return and stay home
in Indiana if he were allowed to see his favorite motion-picture
star in person. The judge, in an indulgent mood, made
arrangements for the boy to meet his favorite "cowboy" and to ride
the actor's famous horse. A month later, the boy returned to
California and appeared again before the judge, this time with
three other transient companions. The boy explained to the judge:
"You see, Judge, my friends didn't believe I met him (the cowboy).
They want to ride on his horse, too." Another boy, from the deep
South, listened to the judge remark: "This is the third and last
time I am going to see you in this court." "What's the matter,
Judge?" the boy responded questioningly, "You going to quit?" 9

To discourage the arrival of these transient children, the
Board of Supervisors met in special session and approved a plan to
establish temporary work camps to help children earn passage home.
The plan carried the endorsement of the juvenile court judge, the
probation officer, and the county forester and fire warden.

In the Los Angeles camp, probation officers and county
forestry employees supervised youths jointly. The program was
felt to be successful, and California enacted legislation in 1935
authorizing other California counties to establish forestry camps
based on the Los Angeles model.10

By 1945 there were eleven court-operated probation camps in
California. To encourage courts to develop local institutions,
California enacted "juvenile homes" legislation in 1945 that
provided state subsidies for the operation of local institutions.11
The legislation included the stipulation that the Youth Authority
would prescribe minimum construction and operation standards.
However, between 1945 and 1957 only five additional local
institutions for juveniles were constructed (see Table 3.2 on
second page following). A Youth Authority consultant points out
that before the subsidy program in 1945, the State Department of
Welfare had considered subsidizing courts for the development of

particular services to help standardize juvenile court practice. As mentioned earlier, however, the Department of Welfare had concluded that subsidies could not overcome the strong localism and fear of state takeover. According to the consultant, "The courts were not ready for it. They did not want any level of state authority such as that which would accompany state subsidization." 12

In 1957, the legislature increased the camp subsidy to include matching state funds for construction as well as funds for operation of local institutions. Courts could qualify for the Camp, Ranch, and School Subsidy of 1957 by meeting the following criteria:13

1. Be established by county ordinance, pursuant to Section 881, Welfare and Institution Code.

2. Have in residence only juvenile court wards on commitment by the juvenile court.

3. Establish a treatment-oriented program designed for children committed for a minimum of thirty consecutive days.

4. Have an identifiable geographic area and programs that are physically separated from other county institutions or programs.

5. Employ separate staff members responsible to the superintendent of the juvenile home, ranch, or camp.

During the next four years the number of court-operated institutions increased from sixteen to thirty-one. From 1960 to 1970, thirty-seven additional facilities were constructed (see Table 3.2 on next page).

The 1957 Camp, Ranch, and School Subsidy Act resulted from a decision by Stark, then Director of the Youth Authority, that

Table 3.2

California's Local Juvenile
Treatment Institutions

Year	Number of Facilities	Youth Capacity
1945	11	690
1955-56	16	975
1960-61	31	2,000
1962-63	41	2,800
1964-65	42	2,894
1966-67	50	3,082
1968-69	54	3,476
1969-70	68	3,677

an increased financial incentive would encourage courts to develop institutions. Stark arrived at this opinion after a series of meetings with the Probation Advisory Committee (a group of California probation officers) and numerous individual discussions with probation officers.

In interviews about Stark's approach in encouraging courts to develop camps and ranches, two Youth Authority consultants indicated that the Probation Advisory Committee served as a sounding board for new ideas or programs pertaining to juvenile court services.[14] Stark attempted to gain consensus by first throwing out the camp idea at general meetings. This action was followed by individual discussions in which Stark put forth the question, "If we could provide a new subsidy, could and would you build local institutions?" The decision to include construction costs in the Subsidy Act was made after probation officers indicated their difficulty in obtaining substantial county funds for court service developments. Therefore, before the 1957 Camp, Ranch, and School Subsidy revision was proposed formally, the Youth Authority and probation officers from a number of counties had agreed that if construction funds were made available, local juvenile courts would be in a much stronger position to gain matching county funds for camps or ranches. Stark's concept of subsidy necessitated preliminary bargaining and minimal state and county consensus. The Youth Authority consultants pointed out that subsidy without these prior conditional agreements would have been "like putting the money on a stump and running like hell."

The bargaining between Stark and the probation officers was another step toward developing state and county consensus on the local institution issue. In effect, this effort involved negotiations that resulted in a conditional agreement that if increased state subsidy was made available, the probation officers would push for the necessary political support to initiate development of local institutions. Stark was well known for his ability to secure legislative approval for various Youth Authority programs and expansions; therefore, many probation officers began their campaigns for political support even before legislative approval of the revised subsidy.

No doubt Stark's probation background influenced the Youth Authority's push for the expansion of local institutions during the 1950s. Stark's career had begun in Los Angeles County probation camps. Throughout his years as Director of the Youth Authority, Stark was known as a believer in community-based corrections. He felt treatment could be accomplished best through the expansion of local juvenile court services.

According to a Youth Authority consultant, a more comprehensive explanation of the Youth Authority's advancement of local institutions lies in a contradiction in that state agency's goals and interests. As discussed before, the original thrust of the Youth Authority was toward researching, developing, and upgrading juvenile court services. However, because of major problems in the state's reformatories in 1945, the Governor requested and the legislature confirmed the Youth Authority to manage the state's reformatories and parole services. This development brought about "a contradiction of interests," which explains why the Youth Authority, in 1957, would advocate local institutional expansion that could, in fact, erode the state's reformatory functions. It is significant that, because of the influence of the Youth Authority, both indirect (delay in state reformatory placements) and direct (Camp, Ranch, and School Subsidy), North County developed a serious commitment to a local institution program.

Quest for Political Support

A local youth institution was first thought about in 1945. North County's argument, which appeared in its 1946 Annual Probation Report, was as follows:

45

At present, there is no in-between facility
available to which delinquent boys twelve
years of age and over can be committed. They
must be in their own homes, on probation, or
with the California Youth Authority.
Although most youth admitted there would be
returned home after a period of five to ten
days, the program should be planned so that
some children could remain there from four to
six months. A very satisfactory site has
been located and the Board of Supervisors has
been requested to buy it. The matter is
under consideration by the Board of
Supervisors. Service clubs and women's
groups are interesting themselves in this
problem. It is believed that they will
strongly support this move.[15]

As previously stated, between 1945 and 1952 it was
increasingly hard for the county to place court wards in state
reformatories because they were overcrowded. This problem was
reflected in increased daily populations in the Juvenile Hall.
Furthermore, the court was committing more youths to state
reformatories (see Table 3.1 on page 41).

These difficulties were acknowledged by both the Superior
Court Judges Committee and the Probation Committee (later to be
called the Juvenile Justice Commission). Support of these two
organizations was sought before any other local support. As a
North County probation officer explained,

If you had a court problem that involved
county financing, you needed the joint
support of all judges. Therefore, you go to
the judges first and air your case. The
judges, who appoint the probation committee,
carry a lot of influence; therefore, if they
agree, the probation committee is likely to
agree as well.[16]

The probation officer summarized the process as one in which

you always go through the appropriate
channels. If you don't, you will be labeled
an empire builder and ultimately lose your
constituency. You have to learn how the
bureaucracy works. I have been criticized
because I am not aggressive enough but there
are times that you can take advantage of
opportunities if you have not developed
enemies. You must be able to expand or

46

contract depending on the political
circumstances or need at hand.[17]

Between 1945 and 1952, this probation officer was able to
establish consensus between the judges and Probation Committee
about the need for a Boys' Center. The question in 1952 was how
to secure broad local support. A joint meeting of the Superior
Court Judges Committee, the Probation Committee, and the probation
officer, decided that setting up a Citizens' Committee to study
the need for a treatment institution would be an appropriate
strategy. It was further determined the committee should include
representatives from several local groups that would support this
type of development and carry considerable influences with the
Board of Supervisors.

Members of the Citizens' Committee as ultimately constituted
included the probation officer, the juvenile court judge, a
Probation Committee member, the Assistant Superintendent of
Schools, a representative of the Federation of Women's Clubs, and
the president of the district PTA. The probation officer
explained that "people were selected whose name meant something to
the Board of Supervisors." According to the probation officer,
the PTA president was chosen because of her known political
influence and interest in the Boys' Center. The women's group had
a history of supporting court service expansions, support based on
the assumption that additional youth services would lead to a
decline in youth problems. The probation officer normally sought
out these groups when court service expansions were proposed.

The Assistant Superintendent of Schools, who chaired the
Committee, had a particular interest in the Boys' Center
development. The county schools were dissatisfied with the
juvenile court's response to truancy, which amounted to home
probation supervision. The probation officer explained to school
officials that serious truants should not be sent to state
reformatories but could be handled by a local institution. With
this in mind, school officials became involved in the supportive
politics for the Boys' Center.[18]

The probation officer pre-determined the Citizen's Committee
activities. He arranged tours to selected counties that were
successfully operating local boys' institutions. The committee
members visited the Juvenile Hall and were familiarized with the
problems in detention conditions that the local institution would
relieve. Those committee members who were not connected directly
with court issues were also informed about a variety of relevant
problems that were said to be connected with the lack of a local
institution, including (1) the rising number of court referrals,
(2) the lack of "adequate" court alternatives for problem youths,
(3) the wait in detention associated with state reformatory
commitments, and (4) the associated over-reliance on home

47

probation supervision. The probation officer attempted to convince committee members of the general need for a local institution and to demonstrate the connection between the Boys' Center and the interests represented by the three members who were not connected directly with the court system.

Ultimately the school administrator supported the Boys' Center because of its potential for deterring and/or treating serious truants. The district PTA has a Juvenile Protection Committee of which the probation officer was a member, that was concerned directly with local youth services. Its function was to provide financial or political support for those youth programs it considered appropriate. Similarly, the Federation of Women's Clubs in its bylaws, specified child welfare as one of its primary functions. Earlier, this group had been responsible for gathering funds for North County's first Juvenile Hall in 1927 and, according to the probation officer, continually involved itself in court service developments. The interaction between the probation officer and these local groups established the necessary consensus for the groups to exert political influence with the Board of Supervisors. Specifically, the local groups' "medium of exchange" to the court was political influence in support of a youth institution. Following the successful "process of familiarization" with the local institution issue, committee members met and discussed how they should present their arguments to the Board of Supervisors. It was decided that each member would argue individually for the Boys' Center. On June 9, 1953, each of the six members spoke before the Board of Supervisors.

The Board of Supervisors responded with agreement. In August, they requested a lease from the federal government for facilities that had once been a part of a military base to be used for the Boys' Center. But the federal government refused, which meant another plan had to be developed. In 1955, the supervisors appropriated $30,000 for the county to purchase a site for a new county branch jail with the intention that the old branch jail site be turned over to the juvenile court for the Boys' Center. Both the court and the sheriff's department found that plan unsatisfactory. The following year the supervisors increased the sum by $45,000 for purchase of a site specifically for the Boys' Center. It was not until 1958 that a satisfactory site could be located and purchased.

To qualify for the Camp, Ranch, and School Subsidy for the Boys' Center, state standards had to be met. The county decided on a three-phase construction plan both to facilitate meeting state subsidy requirements and to allow more time for the county to generate its matching funds. Phase I, to be completed in 1959, would enable the Boys' Center to care for twenty boys. Phase II would increase the capacity by 1960 to forty. Phase III would complete the Boys' Center in 1961 with a sixty-boy capacity.

In summary, North County's development of the Boys' Center reflects, in part, a blurring of the court's organizational needs and youth treatment needs. Because of the scarcity of finances, the need for political support, and the state's subsidy requirements, the court was predisposed to promote the Boys' Center as a means to respond to a variety of local youth concerns and state requirements. This resulted in multiple goals and youth targets for the Boys' Center.

IMPLEMENTATION OF THE
BOYS' CENTER PROGRAM

In 1960, the Boys' Center opened. Its staff, under a superintendent who had been a deputy probation officer with the county since 1952, included two deputy probation officers, three counselors, two cooks, and a secretary. The Boys' Center program was described in the County's 1959 Annual Probation Report as follows:

> In this initial phase the Boys' Center will offer a twenty-four hour program for twenty-one delinquent boys between the approximate ages of fourteen and sixteen years. The program will be a half a day work and half a day school with a strong emphasis on remedial education and group counseling. The Boys' Center will fill a long needed local treatment program for delinquent boys who are not able to adjust in the community and need a twenty-four hour program before further planning can be done on their behalf. The operation of the Boys' Center should provide a reduction in the population of the younger delinquent boys section at the Juvenile Hall, where many boys have been awaiting placements ordered by the Juvenile Court.[19]

The Boys' Center program emphasized training "middle-class" behaviors, including achievement in school and work, table manners, and temper restraint. Swearing and smoking were prohibited. Each boy was expected to pass through stages of progression and undergo weekly evaluations by the entire staff. The principal means of treatment was a therapeutic community (TC) approach in which there were two TC meetings daily in which staff members and boys criticized each other as well as themselves. Self-criticism was presumed essential for rehabilitation. Many staff members felt that the TC meetings were tremendously successful, especially from a group-control standpoint. Most boys, on the other hand, thought of these meetings as

49

"finksessions" in which they were to inform the counselors about wrongdoings they had witnessed or been involved in.

In its early months, several of the youths admitted to the Boys' Center were boys from middle-class families who had experienced difficulty getting along with their parents. For them, its TC approach and middle-class orientation were not difficult to adjust to and may well have been beneficial. However, most Boys' Center clients came from minority or lower-class backgrounds and often experienced significant difficulty fitting into the Boys' Center's regimentation. A number of these youths chose to run away. Once apprehended, they were usually returned to Juvenile Hall and committed to a state reformatory. Even though the Boys' Center pushed state reformatory commitments for their runaways to discourage the practice, boys continued to run away. Many of them indicated that they preferred to go to state reformatories, believing that "state time" was less difficult than time at the Boys' Center.

An "intake committee" selected youths for admission to the Boys' Center. The committee was comprised of the juvenile court's psychologist, the school principals for Juvenile Hall and the Boys' Center, and the superintendent of the Boys' Center. The admission decision process was initiated by a deputy probation officer, who presented information indicating why a youth was appropriate for the Boys' Center. Following this, the intake committee members and deputy probation officers discussed the information, attempting to reach a decision with consensus.

Within several months, the deputy probation officers came to what the Boys' Center superintendent described as "an understanding" of what youths were Boys' Center "client-types." This understanding is reflected in this description of the "client types" published in the County's 1960 Annual Probation Report, less than six months into the operation of the Boys' Center.

> It seems the Boys' Center program is most helpful to boys whose history of delinquency does not extend further back than two to three years. This type of boy seems to adapt himself more readily to the program and is able to gain insight into some of the causes contributing to his delinquency. We have been least helpful to the immature boy who has a long history of deprived emotional life. The latter boy often has difficulty in relating to his peer group and needs a programs of much longer duration.[20]

The initial implementation of the Boys' Center demonstrates an attempt to deal with multiple goals and related client targets.

It is interesting to note that after just six months of operation, conclusions were being drawn about what kinds of youths the Boys' Center could treat most effectively obviously on the basis of their comparative adjustments to the regimentation of the Boys' Center. Lacking the benefit of specific goals and client targets, the Boys' Center in practice was implemented primarily to serve emotionally stable youths with short delinquent histories. Since such youths would not ordinarily have been sent to state reformatories, since those were, in effect, the court's last resort for its most serious wards, the result was that the Boys' Center emerges as a local institutional supplement to state reformatories instead of an alternative to them.

IMPACT OF THE BOYS'
CENTER PROGRAM

The impact assessment used here and in Chapters 4 and 5 is an analysis of North County's statistical patterns of administering justice to juveniles several years before and several years after implementation of the various court reforms.[21] These assessments begin with statistical descriptions of the county's youth population, arrests, court referrals, referrals closed at intake or placed under informal probation, petitions filed, and subsequent court disposition. The figures for youthful population, arrests, court referrals, and petitions filed are included to account for any significant statistical fluctuations that could affect court disposition patterns. However, the impact of the court reforms is examined primarily in relation to court disposition patterns statistically evident before and after each reform.

In Table 3.3 (on next page), mean percentage comparisons for 1957 to 1959 (three years before the Boys' Center opened) and 1960 to 1962 (three years during the Boys' Center operation) are provided for North County's youth population, juvenile arrests, juvenile court intake referrals of delinquent boys' cases, cases closed at intake or placed under informal probation, and court petitions filed on boys' cases. These figures suggest that the boys' cases referred to juvenile court during the Boys' Center operation were less serious than those referred during the three years before the Boys' Center opened. As a result, proportionately more of the referrals were being closed at intake or placed under informal probation, and fewer petitions for juvenile court appearance were being filed. The significance of the increased proportion of juvenile arrests is unclear because the arrest data include girls. Arrest data for boys only were not available.

Table 3.4 (second page following) lists the yearly totals of delinquent boys under some form of court or state control from

1957 to 1962. During the 1960-1962 period, the average proportion of the court's delinquent boys' cases receiving state reformatory control was equivalent to that in the 1957-1959 period, even though the Boys' Center was in operation.

Table 3.3

Youth Population, Arrests, Court Referrals
of Delinquent Boys' Cases, and Subsequent Disposition

| | MEAN | |
	1957-1959	1960-1962
Youthful population, age 10-17	54,654	64,987
Juvenile arrests	7,378	11,453
Percent of youthful population	13.5	17.6
Juvenile court intake referrals (boys' cases)	1,522	1,836
Percent of youthful population	2.8	2.8
Referrals closed at intake or placed under informal probation	797	1,157
Percent of intake referrals	52.4	63.0
Petitions filed in juvenile court	725	679
Percent of intake referrals	47.6	37.0

Table 3.4

Summary Totals of Delinquent Boys' Cases
Under Some Form of Juvenile Court or State
Reformatory Control

	1957	1958	1959	1960	1961	1962
Delinquent boys' cases under control	592	669	665	763	708	764
Delinquent boys' cases receiving some form of juvenile court control other than Boys' Center and state reformatory	533	610	600	690	601	661
Delinquent boys' cases receiving Boys' Center control	---	---	---	17	20	20
Delinquent boys' cases receiving state reformatory control	59	59	65	56	87	83
Proportion of delinquent cases under state reformatory control	0.100	0.089	0.098	0.073	0.123	0.109

Table 3.5 (on next page) provides a percentage measurement of the change in the numbers of delinquent boys receiving state reformatory dispositions during the first three years of the Boys' Center operation. A transitional probability calculation (see Note 22) was used to compute the number of boys expected to be under state reformatory control. A comparison of the expected number with the actual number (three-year mean) resulted in no change; seventy-four were expected to receive and seventy-five actually received state reformatory dispositions. A comparison using an estimated number that excludes the Boys' Center youths with the actual number in state reformatories resulted in a 34.0 percent increase. This comparison demonstrates that, with widening of alternatives created by the opening of the Boys' Center, boys who would have been judged not in need of institutional dispositions were now judged suitable for an institutional disposition within the less constraining institutional framework which that alternative provided. In effect, the court increased its form of control over delinquent boys by institutional net-widening. Institutional net-widening here refers to extending the institutional client reach of the

53

court system beyond state reformatory youth targets to include new youths who probably would not have been subject to state reformatory dispositions prior to the existence of the Boys' Center.

Table 3.5

Comparison of Expected and Estimated Numbers of Delinquent Boys to Receive State Reformatory Dispositions, 1960-1962, with Actual Numbers

	1960-1962 Actual Number of Boys under State Reformatory Control	Difference	Percentage Increase
Expected number of delinquent boys under control at the state reformatory--74	75	---	---
Estimated number of delinquent boys under control at the state reformatory--56	75	+19	34.0

A major question emerges from the impact assessment; does the court's increased use of institutionalization for boys reflect a greater number of boys with more serious problems coming before the court? A breakdown of reasons for the referral of delinquent boys to the court in the period before the Boys' Center opened compared with the period of its first three years of operation indicates that during the latter, there was a lower percentage of referrals for specific delinquent tendencies (602s) and an increase in the percentages of referrals for the predelinquent tendencies (601s). (See Tables 3.6 and 3.7 on next page.) The "delinquent tendency" category refers generally to youths who have difficulty with their parents. The normal response is informal probation or formal home supervision, and, if this fails, placement with a relative or in a foster home. Therefore, with the increase in the number of boys referred for delinquent tendencies during the 1960-1962 period, an increase would be expected in less severe dispositions instead of the reported increase in institutional dispositions.

Table 3.6

Reasons for Referral of Boys' Cases, 1957-1959

	Total Offenses	Delinquent Tendencies	Specific Offenses
1957	1,255	471	784
% of total offenses		37.5	62.5
1958	1,576	560	1,016
% of total offenses		35.5	64.5
1959	1,773	689	1,084
% of total offenses		38.9	61.1
Mean		573	961
Mean percentage		37.3	62.7

Table 3.7

Reasons for Referral of Boys' Cases, 1960-1962

Year	Total Offenses	Delinquent Tendencies	Specific Offenses
1960	1,743	608	1,135
% of total offenses		34.9	65.1
1961	1,916	797	1,119
% of total offenses		41.6	58.4
1962	1,846	786	1,060
% of total offenses		42.6	57.4
Mean		730	1,090
Mean percentage		39.7	60.3

55

Overall, the assessment of the Boys' Center's developmental background, implementation, and impact demonstrates an interrelationship between juvenile court organization in how and why it responds, implements, and shapes the impact of reform programs. When one considers the organizational character of North County's juvenile court, the transformation of the Boys' Center from a state reformatory alternative into an institutional supplement serving a variety of perceived local youth needs and state requirements is understandable. In order to gain support for the Boys' Center, it was necessary for the court to portray it as able to fulfill a variety of youth service needs. The result was that the Boys' Center was implemented with multiple goals and youth targets, which produced the net-widening impact. It will be shown in Chapter 4 that the use of local institutions as supplements instead of alternatives to state reformatories was not limited to North County, but occurred throughout California's juvenile courts. As a result, large and growing state reformatory populations continued and California began efforts to develop and promote a new community correction alternative to state institutions.

1. Interview with North County's director of juvenile institutions.

2. Deutsch, A. Our Rejected Children. Little, Brown and Company, 1947, pp. 118-119.

3. The multiple functions were to ensure presence in court, impress the child with the seriousness of his conduct, allow quieting down, and administer punishment.

4. Governor's Special Study Commission on Juvenile Justice Report. Sacramento: State of California, 1960, p. 72.

5. Lemert, E. M. Social Action and Legal Change: Revolution Within the Juvenile Court. Aldine Publishing Company, 1970, p. 93.

6. North County Annual Probation Report, 1950.

7. North County Annual Probation Report, 1951.

8. This study's statistical data are drawn from North County's annual probation reports and monthly court intake and subsequent youth disposition information on file in the county probation administration offices. Additional data are drawn from the annual Delinquency and Probation in California Statistical Summaries (1957-1972) for the California Youth Authority by the Bureau of Criminal Statistics: State of California.

9. Pezman, T. L. "Untwisting the Twisted." Probation Camps in California. Published by Camps, Ranches, and Schools Division, California Probation, Parole, and Correctional Association, 1963, pp. 1-2.

10. Vaughn, R. "A Century of County Camps." California Youth Authority Quarterly Vol. 17, No. 3 (1964):26-31.

11. For discussion on the growth of county treatment institutions for youths in California see Board of Corrections, Institutions: Correctional Systems Study. State of California (1971), pp. 7-15.

12. Interview with a California Youth Authority consultant under directors Karl Holton, Heman Stark, and Allan Breed.

13. California Welfare and Institutions Code, Article 15, Section 881.

57

14. Interview with two California Youth Authority consultants, one of which was an assistant director for research and development for the Youth Authority during the 1957 Camp, Ranch, and School Subsidy period. The other consultant was affiliated with the Youth Authority's administration during 1957.

15. North County Annual Probation Report, 1946.

16. Interview with North County probation officer.

17. Interview with North County probation officer.

18. Interview with North County probation officer.

19. North County Annual Probation Report, 1959.

20. North County Annual Probation Report, 1960.

21. North County juvenile court's processing of youths begins usually with arrest, which can be followed by either reprimand and release by police or a referral to the court's intake. Most court intake referrals originate from the police but youths can be referred by parents, school, or other sources. Following a referral, court intake personnel can release the youth, place him on informal probation without supervision, or file a petition for court action. At the court hearing the judge can dismiss the case, place the youth on six months home probation without court wardship, or arrive at a formal disposition that varies in relation to the court's available service alternatives.

22. To compute the expected number of delinquent boys to be subject to state reformatory dispositions, a transitional probability was used. The transitional probability is a mean of the proportion of delinquent boys cases under some form of court control receiving state reformatory dispositions during 1957-59. The expected number of boys to receive state reformatory dispositions was computed by multiplying the transitional probability, or 0.10, by the mean of delinquent boys' cases under some form of court control during 1960-1962, or 0.745. Additionally, an estimated number of delinquent boys to be subject to state reformatory dispositions is provided to assess directly the Boys' Center's impact upon the court's use of state reformatory dispositions for delinquent boys. The estimated number was computed by subtracting the 1960-1962 mean of delinquent boys receiving Boys' Center dispositions (19) from the expected number of delinquent boys to be subject to state reformatory dispositions.

CHAPTER 4

PROBATION SUBSIDY

In the early 1960s, California continued to search for ways
to stem its ever growing state reformatory and prison populations.
During this period, the community correction movement was gaining
nationwide momentum. Out of this context, California developed
its probation subsidy program. The program was to provide locally
administered intensive probation service alternatives for youths
and adults formerly subject to state institutions. The community
programs were to be funded by state subsidies. The probation
subsidy program is often referred to as one of the major programs
in the community correction movement.

This chapter focuses upon North County's experiences with
probation subsidy. It is demonstrated that financial earnings
were a major county concern, in its development of the program.
Despite expressed belief in the treatment efficacy of the program,
subsequent program growth and decline were dictated by the
county's subsidy earnings. Much as in the case of the Boys'
Center, probation subsidy is shown to have been implemented with
broad client targets that enabled the court to use the program as
it saw fit. The end result was that the program served both as an
alternative to the state reformatory function and as a supplement
to previous court practice, thereby producing net-widening in
which the court's control over youths was extended.

DEVELOPMENTAL BACKGROUND
OF PROBATION SUBSIDY

The 1957 revision of the 1945 Camp, Ranch, and School Subsidy
Act proved to be a major success in doubling the number of local
youth institutions. However, it became apparent that the local
institutions were not being used as alternatives to state
reformatories. For example, between 1950 and 1963, the Youth
Authority's reformatories expanded rapidly because of increasing
county commitments. In 1964, it was predicted that by 1975 both
the Youth Authority and the adult Department of Corrections would
experience a 100 percent increase in the number of new admissions,
excluding recidivists, despite the newly available local
institutions. Smith states that this expansion pattern would
occur because the state had

> no control over its own client intake, hence
> workloads and expenditures. State
> correctional workloads were directly affected
> by the extent to which county probation was
> used as an alternative for those offenders

who might otherwise be committed to a state
correctional agency.[1]

Since state correction workloads were dictated by each
county, it was felt to be necessary for the state to encourage
counties to reduce their rates of state commitment, thereby
checking the expansion of state institutions. The Youth Authority
had experienced its greatest success at influencing local courts
with the 1957 revision of the Camp, Ranch, and School Subsidy Act.
However, Smith indicates that

> the state had not declared a social policy
> that accepted or publicly acknowledged the
> reciprocal relationship between county
> decisions to treat or not treat locally and
> the consequences of that decision at the
> state level.[2]

Furthermore, counties were not willing to give up any of their
historically guaranteed rights of home rule over court services
despite the problems associated with financing the operation of
various court services and the relief that receipt of state funds
would produce. The importance of this strong "localism" sentiment
and its restrictive role in county and state attempts to reach
agreement on court issues is summarized by Smith as follows:

> County and state efforts to reach agreement
> about ways to improve the probation service
> and standards of performance had snagged over
> the issue of county independence. The fork
> of the dilemma faced by the state was the
> development of standards for county probation
> that build in some uniformity of practice
> without emasculating the county's right and
> responsibility for local decision and action.
> The other fork of the dilemma pointed
> directly at county probation departments who
> recognized the need for improvements in
> quality and quantity of probation services
> but also recognized that this implied the
> acceptance of new standards associated with
> any financial assistance offered by the
> state.[3]

Smith identifies the conflict facing local administrators.
They wanted to take advantage of financial opportunities, but to
do so they had to forsake local autonomy. The benefits of any
state-sponsored program had to be significant before the counties
would disregard their localism sentiment.

Intensive Probation
Supervision

The Youth Authority initiated research in 1961 to document
empirically the rehabilitative usefulness of less expensive
community treatment programs as alternatives to state
reformatories. Phase I of the research, the "Community Treatment
Project," involved a comparative study of the rehabilitative
effectiveness of reformatories as compared to intensive
community-based probation supervision programs. Selected
subgroups of one geographical area's delinquent population were
studied. Marguerite Warren, a project researcher, describes the
experiment as follows:

> The intake cases are first identified as
> eligible or ineligible for the
> community-based program. Approximately
> ninety percent of girls and seventy percent
> of boys have been declared as eligible, with
> the primary reason for exclusion being
> assaultive behavior. Eligible cases are then
> randomly assigned to institutional and
> community programs. The research design
> calls for following both those cases assigned
> to the traditional Youth Authority program
> (the Controls) and those cases assigned to
> the community program (the Experimentals), in
> terms of personal and attitude change as
> reflected in psychological tests given before
> and after intensive treatment.[4]

After several years, research findings indicated that when
total experimental and total control cases were compared, there
was

> a considerable advantage to the
> community-based program for all delinquent
> sub-types combined as indicated both in
> parole behavior criteria and in test-score
> changes.[5]

However, these findings which indicated higher rehabilitative
success for the intensive community treatment approach, did not
identify which approach or combination of approaches accounted for
the increased success among particular youth subgroups.
Nonetheless, as Warren points out, "the feasibility of treating a
large proportion of the juvenile offender population in intensive
community programs, rather than institutions, was a settled
issue."[6]

61

Four substudies followed the Phase I study, to further specify the desirability of community treatment compared to state institutionalization. On the basis of what they found, the state claimed that at least 25 percent of the new admissions to the Department of Corrections and the Youth Authority in 1964 could safely have remained in the community with good home supervision.[7]

The concept emerging at the state level was that community supervision was a feasible alternative to the state's institutional methods. As a Youth Authority consultant states,

> While the community-treatment data were irrelevant and inconclusive since they did not specify the particular community-treatment methods that would yield greater rehabilitative results, they did provide a potential solution to the state's expansion crisis in corrections.[8]

The state's problem was deciding what form of subsidy to use to gain broad community interest and support for this new community correction program.

The initial subsidy proposals included (1) complete state subsidization of all court services, (2) state contracts for special probation services from the counties, (3) a salary subsidy to enable counties to increase probation staff and decrease caseloads, (4) a postcommitment subsidy in which selected cases committed to the state would be returned to the courts and placed on probation, and (5) a subsidy based on county performance in reducing their state commitments and developing intensive probation supervision programs.

Probation Subsidy and the Quest for Local Participation

The probation subsidy program efforts began in 1964 with the establishment of a State Planning Committee. This committee was responsible for developing the intensive community supervision idea into an understandable program that would appeal to a broad range of local and state interests. It included a member of the research study team for intensive probation supervision, the Chief of the Youth Authority's Division of Delinquency Prevention, the Executive Officers for the Board of Corrections, a Sacramento State College statistician, and two representatives from the Youth Authority's Research and Development Division.[9] At their first meeting, the administrator of the State Youth and Adult Correction Agency informed the committee that because 1964 was a budget year rather than a policy year in the California legislature, the legislature would consider only a program that did not involve an increase in state expenditures. Therefore, the committee needed a program that clearly demonstrated no increase in state spending. The idea that emerged from the initial meeting was "if what we want to do is keep people out of the state system, why not pay counties not to commit them." [10] The question was how the state would determine equitable county payments.

Following the initial meeting, Youth Authority representatives worked on developing a financial formula based upon their career costs of institutionalizing and providing successful parole services for committed youths. The concern was to develop "rock bottom state career costs" that would provide base figures from which the state's county reimbursement could be derived. A prevailing assumption was that counties could work with five to six persons for the same amount that the state would spend on one because the counties would not rely on institutionalization. The ultimate formula involved correlating three variables: (1) the state's goal of a 25 percent reduction in the counties' commitment of youths and adults to state institutions, (2) the county average rate of commitment of offenders to the state per 100,000 population during the past five years, and (3) the dollar amount granted to counties for decreases in their base commitment rate. Counties were to receive from $2,080 to $4,000 per case depending on the percent of decrease between the base commitment rates and current commitment rates.[11]

Once the formula was determined, the proposed program was presented to Youth Authority personnel and probation officers. The Youth Authority advanced the probation subsidy plan to appropriate state and county groups before submitting the bill to the legislature.

Because the members of the Probation Officer's Association were divided on the bill, there was a weekend meeting between Youth Authority personnel and county probation officers where they attempted to negotiate the probation subsidy earnings. Ultimately the probation officers decided that "since the bill was going to fly in the legislature," they would support it and together they and the Youth Authority could work out the funding flaws later.[12]

The Youth Authority's subsequent approach in promoting subsidy included contacts with state legislators, judges, boards of supervisors, and so on. Their primary message was the potential financial gain for both the state and the counties. Further contacts were made with such interest groups as the California Congress of Parents and Teachers Associations, the Federation of Women's Clubs, California Taxpayer's Associations, Juvenile Officers' Associations, the National Council on Crime and Delinquency, and other fraternal and social service organizations. Support from these organizations was sought both for the probation subsidy legislation and later for implementation of the program in individual counties. The Youth Authority was in a strong bargaining position, even though the agencies with which it was dealing represented a variety of organizational concerns. Arguments for probation subsidy included its cost effectiveness, increased humanitarianism, and increased rehabilitation success.

The promotion process for probation subsidy began with training selected Youth Authority personnel to deliver lectures and slide presentations designed for simple explanation of the program benefits. Smith writes:

> Because of the complexity of the legislation, some means had to be found to present this new subsidy concept clearly and intelligently to the Governor, State Legislators, the State Supervisors Association, private citizen groups, correctional organizations and associations, boards of supervisors, panels of judges, and probation officers themselves. Initially, the public information and educational program conducted by the Youth Authority designed to sell the subsidy program, utilized conventional charts and graphs. These were found to be impractical for large groups, and a better means had to be devised. At the encouragement of the Youth Authority's artist, slides and transparencies for an overhead portable projector were developed. With the assistance of Youth Authority staff, slides were constructed dealing with the various aspects of subsidy. All verbal and graphic presentations were designed to make a simple and clear presentation of the proposal to groups representing various levels of sophistication and knowledge about the correctional process and the needs of a good probation service. Aside from promoting support, this educational campaign was also designed to neutralize potential opposition before it arose. As a result, organizations that might have opposed the subsidy plan were the first to be contacted and informed about the proposal being advanced by the State Board of Corrections.[13]

The probation subsidy program was supported by various local and state groups, partly because they interpreted it as a way to save money. By participating, counties could receive substantial state funds that could be used to offset their increasing budgets. The state did not reimburse the counties, however, until supervision services were being provided. The exchange agreements between the state and the county were based on county performance; the legislation of the probation subsidy stipulated that the medium of exchange included both commitment rate reduction and corresponding operation of local intensive probation services.

Probation Subsidy
Legislation

Ultimately the probation subsidy program was the result of (1) a perceived state expansion crisis in both youth and adult correction institutions, (2) the state's development of an alternate plan to state institutionalization that was appealing to a range of state and county interests, and (3) a successful campaign by the Youth Authority that resulted in the state and county consensus necessary to implement the new program. The specific legislation for probation subsidy was divided into seven sections.[14] The sections stipulated the legislation's intent (Section 1820), the state sharing of cost (Section 1821), the establishment of minimum standards by the Youth Authority (Section 1822), the stipulation that the county and the Youth Authority would develop cooperatively standards and procedures for probation subsidy units (Section 1823), county application for funds (Section 1824), the approval of application and determination of fund reimbursement (Section 1825, (a) through (i)), and the Youth Authority's periodic reports to the legislature on subsidy program experiences and results (Section 1826).

A primary area of controversy in the probation subsidy legislation was what role the Youth Authority was to play in approving county applications for state funds, the calculation of commitment rate reduction, and financial reimbursement (all of which fall under Section 1824). The legislation clearly indicated that counties would not be entitled to probation subsidy funds unless the minimum subsidy standards were met. Section 1824, Subsection (a) states:

> No county shall be entitled to receive any state funds provided by this article until its application is approved and unless and until the minimum standards prescribed by the Department of Youth Authority are complied with and then only on such terms as are set forth hereafter in this section.

Subsections (b), (c), and (d) of Section 1825 are concerned with calculation of case commitment, annual commitment rate, and reimbursement for commitment rate reduction. Subsection (3) prescribes the method of reimbursement:

The state will reimburse the county upon presentation of a valid claim based on actual performance in reducing the commitment rate from its base rates. Whenever a claim made by a county, pursuant to this article, covering a prior fiscal year is found to be in error, adjustment may be made on a current claim without the necessity of applying the adjustment to the allocation for the prior year.

Subsection (f) stipulates that if the amount computed under Subsection (d) is less than the maximum, the differences can be used the following fiscal year. This provision enabled counties to count on unused funds for future programs. Subsection (g) further states:

In the event a participating county earns less than the sum paid in the previous year because of extremely unusual circumstances claimed by the county and verified by the Director of the Youth Authority, with the approval of the Director of Finance, the Director of the Youth Authority may pay to the county a sum equal to the prior year's payment provided, however, that in subsequent years the county will be paid only the amount earned.

Subsection (1) specifies that probation subsidy funds cannot be used to support existing county probation programs or to expand local institutions for youths. Subsidy funds were to be used to develop intensive probation services for youths who would have been committed to state reformatories if these services had not been available.

Subsections (f) and (g), amendments to the original probation subsidy legislation, represent specific compromises between the state and the counties. The counties were interested in receiving state finances with no state control over how the funds were used. As the legislation was initially written, if a county operated intensive probation programs at a cost lower than their earnings, the remaining earnings had to be returned to the state. An emergency change was made in Subsection (f) of the probation subsidy legislation to guarantee the county its surplus earnings up to one year if its intensive probation program continued to operate at a level equal to that represented by the reserved funds. Subsection (g) was another extended financial provision for counties. In cases where circumstances resulted in increased state commitments, the level of intensive probation programming could continue at the previous year's level.

Under Subsection (h) the state was able to ensure specific county use of probation subsidy funds. State law prohibits the payment of subsidies twice for the same county probation service. The addition of Subsection (h) as mentioned earlier, stipulated that probation subsidy earnings could not be spent on expanding or developing local institutions. The state was not opposed to county expansion of local institutions, but it did not want to be involved in a double subsidy practice in which counties would receive money for reduced state commitments, and then place the diverted youths in an institution whose construction and operation costs were financed substantially under California's Camp, Ranch, and School Subsidy. For similar reasons, Section 1824 required counties to submit their plans for intensive probation units to the Youth Authority, which reviewed them to ensure compliance with probation subsidy program standards before intensive probation operations were initiated. Section 1824 also provided for Youth Authority audits of the programs during their operation.

A major county criticism of probation subsidy involved the specification that county subsidy earnings must be used only for intensive probation. Nonetheless, even with the spending specifications for probation subsidy the counties managed to juggle their subsidy spending to facilitate a variety of court expansions that were not limited to intensive probation services. Smith points out that through "funding manipulations," some probation departments have used their probation subsidy to offset the cost of their normal growth. In some instances, according to Smith, the subsidy earnings have encouraged counties to make excessive expenditures to take full advantage of their earnings. In effect, counties let their subsidy earnings dictate court services expansions.[15]

North County's Response to Probation Subsidy

The probation officer of North County was opposed to the probation subsidy bill at first. As he stated,

> I didn't like the bill. First, the way it
> was originally drawn up, you had to commit
> county funds to begin intensive probation
> supervision programs before you were able to
> receive reduction earnings; and second, you
> had to spend these earnings each year.[16]

With these objections in mind, the probation officer successfully led several other probation officers in negotiating with Youth Authority personnel and Youth Authority Director Stark, to amend the legislation so counties could receive quarterly reimbursements to finance intensive probation units.

To begin adapting North County's court services toward participation in the probation subsidy program, the probation officer presented his general views and specific strategies to the Superior Court Judges Committee. The probation officer recalled,

> It was not a case where I went before the judges and said we should stop committing to state institutions so we can earn $4,000 per case. My argument was that our state commitment rates of adults and juveniles had generally been to high and now that this state money was available we could gain financing that would help us expand our local court service programs and lower our caseloads.[17]

The court's strategy for implementing probation subsidy programs was cautious. Only one small program was developed during the first year. Subsequent program developments were to be dictated by the court's subsidy earnings. The probation officer explained that this gradual program implementation approach resulted from his status as a county official; "My concern was with going into the program and coming out okay financially."[18] After the meeting with the Superior Court judges, the probation officer arranged for a Youth Authority representative to conduct an informational meeting about the probation subsidy program. Those invited included the juvenile court judges, members of the Juvenile Justice Commission, and selected probation personnel. The meeting provoked an extensive debate between the Youth Authority representative and the county auditor, who was concerned with potential costs to the county resulting from court participation in the subsidy program.

The final decision on participation in probation subsidy lay with the Board of Supervisors. They were generally disillusioned with state and federal programs that initiated new local services. According to the probation officer, local officials were always concerned that outside funds, though they could help start programs, could also be withdrawn, resulting in either increased county expenditures for continued operation or a cutback in programs. Therefore the Board of Supervisors wanted assurance that if North County was to participate in the program, the subsidy additions (intensive probation units) would not require county funds. The County Administrator suggested to the Board of Supervisors that it should request a legal interpretation of the Probation Subsidy Act from the County Counsel. The probation officer presented a plan for program implementation in which the county's financial risks were low. First, a conservative estimate of county subsidy earnings for reduced commitments during 1966 to 1967 was several times the $66,144 cost for the first intensive probation unit to be developed. Second, the county would transfer one probation officer supervisor and three deputy probation officers into the unit but not have to hire any new deputy probation officers, meaning that the Board of Supervisors would not be required to increase the probation department's budget. On the basis of this gradual implementation plan and a favorable interpretation of the legislation of the subsidy program by the County Counsel, the Board of Supervisors approved the plan.

Subsequent development and/or reduction of intensive probation units was to be dictated by the county's subsidy earnings. In fact, because of a decline in subsidy earnings, the county did cut back on its intensive probation programs during 1971, terminating three of the units (two adult and one juvenile). The state commitment increases which produced the subsidy declines, primarily involved juveniles. Indeed, one juvenile court judge demonstrated a strong tendency during this period to commit juveniles to state institutions and ignore the alternative intensive probation services.

North County claimed that its intensive probation units were successful in reducing recidivism. The County's 1968 Annual Probation Report states, "In the juvenile units only five minors have been committed to the California Youth Authority from the intensive units from 1967 to 1968."[19] Nonetheless, even with the perceived success of intensive probation, the county was not willing to maintain the programs without total state funding.

What emerged from North County's response to probation subsidy was an overriding concern for the financing of the programs. Philosophically, with the exception of one juvenile court judge, the county appeared in agreement with the state concerning the youth treatment benefits of intensive probation over state reformatories. However, the county continued to feel the state should bear all program costs. As a result, despite the county's expressed belief in the rehabilitative efficacy of the programs, its initial development, expansion, and reduction of intensive probation programs was in direct relation to its subsidy earnings.

IMPLEMENTATION OF THE PROBATION
SUBSIDY PROGRAM

In 1967, North County established two intensive home probation units for juveniles. During the same year, the court initiated two day-care programs for delinquent girls (Girls' Guide) one of which received its funding from probation subsidy earnings, the other from Camp, Ranch, and School Subsidy funds. The two juvenile intensive probation units handled both boys and girls. Girls' Guide programs were for girls with particular problems in adjusting to public schools. The intensive probation

69

units and Girls' Guide operated in separate facilities, each unit handling its own intake of cases and program treatment.

The probation subsidy legislation required that all participants in intensive probation programs be youths eligible for a state reformatory commitment. Intake of cases into the court's intensive supervision units was guided, but not determined, by this requirement. North County's intensive probation caseloads were comprised primarily of youths who had had problems while on regular court probation. If a deputy probation officer with a regular caseload had a case he or she felt could be handled more suitably by intensive probation, the case could be referred to the intensive unit for intake screening. When the program began, according to the intensive probation supervisors, the screening involved the unit supervisor and the unit's deputy probation officers who made the intake decision as a group. The supervisor stated, "The primary requisite for admission into the unit was an expressed willingness on the part of at least one of the unit's deputy probation officers to work with the youth."[20] Therefore, the tendency was to match a youth with a particular deputy probation officer. If this was not possible, generally the youth was not admitted to the unit.

The intensive probation units very soon found it necessary to require parental consent for participation before accepting a youth into the program. A North County Annual Probation Report stated:

> One or more intensive supervision unit deputies is assigned to read the case to determine the appropriateness of the referral, then a decision is made as to which deputy will interview the youngster and his family. The deputy referring the case may be contacted anytime during the screening process to assist in the understanding of the case. After interviewing the youngster and his family a decision is made whether or not to bring the case into the unit. If the child or his family is strongly against being referred to the intensive supervision unit the chances of our successfully working with the case are nil.[21]

In the treatment of youths, the intensive units used a variety of counseling methods, including family counseling, individual counseling, group counseling, tutoring, crafts, and recreational activities. Youths were normally seen about one hour every two weeks. Parents of a youth were seen somewhat less frequently. An intensive probation officer's caseload averaged fifteen cases, which allowed time for longer and more frequent client contacts. In a comparative study of time spent with probationers and their families in North County, it was determined that the intensive probation officers spent two to three hours per month per youth compared to an average of fifteen minutes per youth on a regular court probation caseload. [22]

Youths who were referred, but not admitted, to the intensive probation units could be referred to the Boys' Center, a group home, a private institution, or (in an extreme case) a state reformatory. Usually, some alternative was used so youths were not committed to state reformatories. An intensive probation supervisor summarized this "something other than state reformatory" trend by stating,

> Our approach was something besides the state. The Boys' Center took some of our rejects and we took some of their rejects. Once the state was knocked off as an alternative, we had to make administrative adjustments. [23]

Consequently, through North County's implementation of intensive probation programs, there was not a direct displacement of youths from state reformatories into the intensive supervision programs. Instead, the tendency was toward accommodating youths displaced from state reformatories locally in various court service alternatives.

IMPACT OF THE PROBATION
SUBSIDY PROGRAM

The major impact question to be considered is how the participation of North County's juvenile court in probation subsidy influenced the way it processed youths. Presumably probation subsidy should result in the court's displacement of youths from state reformatories into intensive probation programs.

Table 4.1 (on next page) provides mean percentage comparisons of the county's youthful population, juvenile arrests, court intake referrals, and subsequent court handling three years before and three years after the implementation of probation subsidy. Referrals either closed at intake or placed under informal probation increased during the 1966-1968 period. Petitions filed for court appearance also declined. The increase in referrals closed or placed under informal probation suggests that at intake the court may have been screening away youths who would have had petitions filed previously or that the cases referred were not serious. This could account for the smaller number of petitions filed.

Table 4.1

County Youth Population, Arrests, Court
Referrals, and Subsequent Disposition

| | MEAN | |
	1963-1965	1966-1968
Youthful population age 10-17	76,041	83,469
Juvenile arrests	14,372	14,539
Percent of youthful population	18.9	17.4
Juvenile court intake referrals	2,873	4,169
Percent of youthful population	3.8	5.0
Referrals closed at intake or placed under informal probation	1,884	2,886
Percent of intake referrals	65.6	69.2
Petitions filed in juvenile court	989	1,283
Percent of intake	34.4	30.8

Summary totals of delinquent cases receiving some form of court service from 1963 to 1968 are provided in Table 4.2 (on next page). There was significant decrease in cases receiving state reformatory dispositions during the 1966-1968 period, reflecting the county's initial involvement in the probation subsidy program. Furthermore, an increasing number of youths were receiving intensive probation services, reflecting the county's "earn and implement" approach to probation subsidy.

Measurement of probation subsidy's impact on the courts use of state reformatories are presented in Table 4.3 (second page following). Using a transitional probability, the number of youths expected to receive state reformatory dispositions was computed for the 1966-1968 period. A comparison of the number expected with the number actually receiving reformatory dispositions showed a decline of 55.0 percent, consistent with the official purpose of probation subsidy. However, when the number of youths it was estimated would be subject to state reformatories--which included the cases receiving intensive probation--is compared with the actual number subject, there is a 35.0 percent increase in the combined total of youths subject to state reformatories and intensive probation. These findings indicate that the overall impact of probation subsidy on the court's pattern of administering services to youths extends beyond the intended displacement of youths from the state's reformatories to the unexpected result of including other youths in intensive probation, youths who were previously handled by some other form of court service.

In assessing the impact of the Boys' Center on the court's administration of services to juveniles, it was concluded that the Boys' Center impact resulted in "institutional net-widening." Probation subsidy's intensive probation was intended as a local court service alternative to state reformatories. Probation subsidy's targeted youths were those previously subject to state reformatory commitments by the court. However, as the preceding findings demonstrate, intensive probation was provided to a number of youths who would not, in all likelihood, previously have been subject to state reformatory commitments. In effect, the availability of intensive probation programs widened North County juvenile court's local net of probation supervision over youths. Though specific legislation established clear client targets for intensive probation programs, a number of nontargeted youths were selected for the new program alternatives. The result was net-widening. Here, as in the case of the Boys' Center, court control over adjudicated youths appears to be extended by the implementation of court reforms.

73

Table 4.2

Summary Totals of Delinquent Cases Under
Some Form of Juvenile Court or State
Reformatory Control

	1963	1964	1965	1966	1967	1968
Delinquent cases under control	1,254	1,364	1,408	1,559	1,637	1,670
Delinquent cases receiving some form of juvenile court control other than intensive home supervision and state reformatory	1,131	1,227	1,287	1,459	1,451	1,438
Delinquent cases receiving intensive home supervision	----	----	----	16	123	171
Delinquent cases receiving state reformatory control	123	137	121	84	63	61
Proportion of delinquent cases under state reformatory control	0.098	0.100	0.086	0.054	0.038	0.036

Table 4.3

Comparison of Expected and Estimated Numbers
of Delinquent Cases Under State Reformatory
Control, 1966-1968, with Actual Number Under
State Reformatory Control [24]

	1966-1968 Mean of Actual Number of Youths Under State Reformatory Control	Difference	Percentage Change
Expected number of youths to be under control in the state reformatory--154	69	-85	-55.0
Estimated number of youths to be under control in the state reformatory--51	69	+18	+35.0

In summary, the development by North County juvenile court of intensive probation services under probation subsidy reflected an "earn and implement" orientation. In implementing the new program, the court altered the way it had previously handled troubled youths so that the use of state reformatories was, in effect, terminated. The result was that court services and control administered to North County youths was both modified and increased, because not only intended state reformatory youths but unintended youths (those not likely to receive state reformatory placements) received intensive probation, the effect being net-widening.

The question is why both the Boys' Center and probation subsidy resulted in net-widening? Clearly, the occurrence of this phenomenon does not mean that the court is concerned solely with its organizational needs and extending its services and/or control over youths. Rather the pattern appears to be indicative of the court's tendency to blur the distinction between organizational goals and interests and the goals and interests of appropriate youth treatment, ends which are often in conflict. This blurred perception leads to the court handling of youths in ways that are expeditious, financially rewarding, and presumedly professional but not necessarily in the youths' best interests. The potential for detrimental effect on these youths from receiving "reform services," particularly for kinds of youths who have not previously been subject to service, will be addressed in the next several chapters.

1. Smith, R.L. A Quiet Revolution: Probation Subsidy. U.S. Department of Health, Education and Welfare. Publication No. (SRS) 72-26011, 1971, p. 7.

2. Smith, pp. 7-8.

3. Smith, p. 10.

4. Warren, M. "The Case for Differential Treatment of Delinquents." In H.L. Voss (ed.), Society, Delinquency and Delinquent Behavior. Little, Brown, and Company, 1970, p. 420.

5. Warren, p. 420.

6. Warren, p. 420.

7. Davis, G. "A Study of Adult Probation Violation Rates by Means of the Cohort Approach." The Journal of Criminal Law and Criminology and Police Science March, 1964.

8. Interview with the California Youth Authority assistant director for research and development who was involved in the state's research, development, and implementation of probation subsidy.

9. Interview with the California Youth Authority assistant director for research and development.

10. Interview with the California Youth Authority assistant director for research and development.

11. Interview with the California Youth Authority assistant director for research and development.

12. Interview with the California Youth Authority assistant director for research and development and the North County probation officer.

13. Smith, p. 29.

14. California Law Relating to Youthful Offenders, Article 7. State Aid for Probation Services, Sections 1820-1826. Department of the Youth Authority, 1970.

15. Smith, pp. 85-87.

16. Interview with North County probation officer.

17. Interview with North County probation officer.

18. Interview with North County probation officer.

19. North County Annual Probation Report, 1968.

20. Interviews with North County's intensive probation supervisors and intensive probation officers for the probation subsidy program.

21. North County Annual Probation Report, 1968.

22. Interviews with North County's intensive probation supervisors and intensive probation officers for the probation subsidy program.

23. Interview with a North County intensive probation supervisor.

24. As in the previous chapter, to compute the expected number of delinquent youths to be subject to state reformatory control during probation subsidy's first three years of operation, a transitional probability was used. In this case, the transitional probability is a mean of the proportion of delinquent youths under some form of court control receiving state reformatory control during 1963-1965. The expected number of youths to be under state reformatory control was computed by multiplying the transitional probability or .095 by the mean of delinquent youths under some form of court control during 1966-1968 or 1,622. Additionally, an estimated number of delinquent youths to be subject to state reformatory control is provided to directly assess the impact of probation subsidy upon the county's use of the state reformatories for delinquent youths. The estimated number was computed by substracting the 1966-1968 mean of delinquent youths receiving probation subsidy's intensive home supervision (103) from the expected number of delinquent youths to be subject to placement in state reformatories.

CHAPTER 5

DIVERSION

The Boys' Center and probation subsidy were officially promoted as providing juvenile courts with local treatment service alternatives to state reformatories. In contrast, diversion was aimed at providing various forms of local treatment alternatives to the juvenile court. Consequently, diversion, like the previous reforms, represents an integral part of the community correction movement aimed at expanding local youth treatment services. However, given its primary purpose of reducing the use of the juvenile court for most troubled youths, diversion departs significantly from the previous reforms.

In its consideration of North County's diversion efforts, this chapter documents the fact that diversion actually shares most of the characteristics of the program development, implementation, and impact of the Boys' Center and probation subsidy. As with the earlier reforms, North County juvenile court's response to diversion was to implement it as a court service supplement for many youths not previously handled by the court, and one which involved their siblings and parents as well. As a result, the net-widening effect of diversion exceeds the impact of the two previous reforms and has several other alarming implications.

THE 1960s: A CRISIS IN JUVENILE JUSTICE

In 1967, the President's Crime Commission was charged with drafting

> a plan for social change responsive to the most authoritative statements concerning the problem of crime in modern America. A major purpose was to focus public attention on a balanced assessment of the weakness of present law and procedure.[1]

One of the commission's most widely discussed proposals called for the "diversion" of selected problem youths from the juvenile court into youth service bureaus.[2] The youth service bureau proposal reflected the commission's desire to substantially narrow the juvenile court's jurisdiction and divert most troubled youths from the official juvenile court system. The proposal reflected a recognition of the juvenile court's failure to meet its prevention, individualized treatment, and rehabilitation goals despite various efforts aimed at expanding and localizing its youth services.[3]

The commission concluded that further infusion of the court with resources would not help it reach its original goal of providing individualized treatment and rehabilitation for troubled youths, and connected the failure to reach that goal with unrealistic expectations based on a

> grossly over-optimistic view of what is known
> about the phenomenon of juvenile criminality
> and of what even a fully equipped juvenile
> court could do about it.[4]

The commission maintained that juvenile correction experts were in agreement that it was very difficult to develop methods to prevent delinquent acts through rehabilitation programs because the delinquency phenomenon was so little understood. Though theories of delinquency offered various explanations, the commission concluded that attempts to understand the causes of delinquency remained inconclusive. [5]

Historically, the juvenile court's overly optimistic view of the causes of youthful criminality and what can prevent or correct it had served as a basis for extending official court control. Yet much official court action could do more harm than good. The underlying assumption had been that official juvenile justice agencies such as the police, juvenile court, probation, and correction institutions can create or support delinquency by their mere contact with youths. As the commission argued:

> Official action may actually help to fix and
> perpetuate delinquency in the child through a
> process in which the individual begins to
> think of himself as delinquent and organizes
> his behavior accordingly. That process
> itself is further reinforced by the effect of
> the labeling upon the child's family,
> neighbors, teacher, and peers, whose
> reactions communicate to the child in subtle
> ways a kind of expectation of delinquent
> conduct. The undesirable consequences of
> official treatment are heightened in programs
> that rely on institutionalizing the child.
> The most informed and benign institutional
> treatment of the child, even in well designed
> and staffed reformatories and training
> schools, thus may contain within it the seeds
> of its own frustration and itself may often
> feed the very disorder it is designed to
> cure.[6]

Even with these criticisms of the juvenile court, the commission did not recommend either a relocation of juvenile court functions or its abolition but argued for a revision of the juvenile court's philosophy toward "more reachable goals." The commission said in summary that the juvenile court's reach had exceeded its grasp, which had led to philosophical and operational discrepancies, and concluded:

> In theory the court's operations could justifiably be informal, its findings and decisions made without observing ordinary procedural safeguards, because it would act only in the best interest of the child. In fact it frequently does nothing more nor less than deprive a child of liberty without due process of law--knowing not what else to do and needing, whether admittedly or not, to act in the community's interest even more imperatively than the child's. In theory it was to exercise its protective powers to bring an errant child back in the fold. In fact there is increasing reason to believe that its intervention reinforces the juvenile's unlawful impulses. In theory, it was to concentrate on each case the best of current social science learning. In fact it has often become a vested interest in its turn, loathe to cooperate with innovative programs or avail itself of forward-looking methods.[7]

Based on the discrepancy between its philosophy and its operation, the commission argued that the juvenile court should alter its philosophy and goals so they do not "outrun reality."

The commission reasoned that ultimately the juvenile court, as a court of law, is charged with protecting the community against threatening conduct. While rehabilitation through individualized handling of problem youths is one way of providing community protection, the court's jurisdiction should be narrowed to only "those cases of manifest danger."[8] It recommended that problem youths who are not imminent risks to the community but are in need of redirection should be screened away from the court and receive prejudicial dispositions into agencies outside the formal juvenile justice system, agencies which could include mental health agencies, social agencies, school guidance units, family counseling services, and other community services.

The diversion of youths from the juvenile court into community youth services was to be carried out by what the commission termed "youth service bureaus." It recommended that

communities should establish neighborhood
youth serving agencies, youth service
bureaus, located if possible in comprehensive
neighborhood community centers and receiving
both delinquent and non-delinquent youth.[9]

While the cases could be referred by parents, schools, or other
sources, most referrals would originate from the police and court
intake. If, after study, certain youths were determined unlikely
to benefit from its services, the bureau could notify the referral
source of its decision not to handle the particular case. The
bureau's primary function would be to provide individually
tailored service for youths in trouble. The commission reasoned
that this individual service could include

group, individual, and family counseling;
placement in group or foster homes; work and
recreational programs; employment counseling;
and special educational services (remedial
and vocational). The coordination of the
youth and his family to the service agency
would be under the direct control of the
bureau, the key to success being the
voluntary participation by the youth and his
family in following the rehabilitation plan.[10]

The purposes of the youth service bureaus were to avoid
stigma for child and family, to rely on more appropriate local
agencies for problem youths, and to energize community
involvement. Margaret Rosenheim suggests that these goals are
very much a part of the long-practiced middle-class approach to
juvenile problems:

Middle-class parents not only work to develop
the social utilities of a good life (e.g.,
Boy Scouts, community centers with youth
programs, good schools with strong supporting
services) but they also invest their energies
individually and vigorously to head off the
risk of stigma attached to their own precious
children, when and if their children run
afoul with authority. They are sensitive and
quick to react to unlawful behavior by
officials. Middle-class parents are also
aided by their ability to tap alternatives to
official legal intervention into the lives of
their children. Many of them are so
positioned as to be able to "buy a little
time" at camp, to enroll a youngster in a
remedial reading class, to arrange a school
transfer through cajolery (sometimes even

82

threat!), to send a child out-of-town to
military academy or to Aunt Jane's for a
period, or, in the case of pregnant
daughters, to arrange discreetly for abortion
or adoption in a distant place. But these
alternatives are unavailing to children of
the poor, largely because the money needed to
secure them is unavailable.[11]

Diversion's youth service bureaus emerge as youth and family
service agencies delivering a variety of services in place of
juvenile court processing to youths normally referred to the
juvenile court system.[12] The primary goal of the bureaus was to
be to help youths solve their problems without subjecting them to
the stigmatizing effects presumed to be associated with juvenile
court contact. The commission, in providing the general concept
of the youth service bureau, did not specify how the bureaus were
to accomplish their tasks, but left their organization and
implementation to the state or the local communities interested in
establishing them.[13]

California's Response
to Diversion

California's diversion approach reflected the recommendation
of the President's Crime Commission. William Underwood, in an
article pertaining to California's establishment of diversion and
youth service bureaus, points out that Howard Ohmart of the
California Youth Authority was a staff member and contributing
author of the commission, and writes:

Upon returning to California, Mr. Ohmart
reported the events of his eighteen months'
work with the National Crime Commission (the
President's Crime Commission). The
recommendation which attracted the most
interest and support related to the
establishment of Youth Service Bureaus.
Former Youth Authority Director, Heman Stark
stimulated interest in behalf of developing
the diversion concept into statewide
practice. Individuals who began moving
diversion into practice included Senator
George Deukmejian of Long Beach; Sheriff Mike
Canlis, San Joaquin County; and members of
the California Delinquency Prevention
Commission.[14]

After reading the commission report, Stark stated that he
wanted California to be the first state to implement diversion.

To promote support for diversion in the state, Stark decided that a law enforcement official should write the first article arguing for the local development of diversion programs and their potential use by law enforcement. In 1968, Michael Canlis, the Sheriff of San Joaquin County and a member of the California Delinquency Prevention Commission, wrote such an article and indicated the urgent need for California to move ahead with diversion programs. Canlis argued that much of what was needed to establish diversion programs could be accomplished within the framework of existing resources through realignment of public and private services and without an increase in state or local funding.[15]

Later in the year, two Youth Authority research personnel and State Senator George Deukmejian wrote a diversion bill which became titled the "Youth Service Bureau Act." Senator Deukmejian introduced the legislation (Senate Bill 892) on April 5, 1968. It detailed the organization and functions of youth service bureaus. Included were state funding provisions to establish four local pilot bureaus that would be required to meet the program guidelines to be established by the California Delinquency Prevention Commission. The Youth Service Bureau Act (Section 1900-1905 of the California Welfare and Institutions Code) was passed by both the Assembly and the Senate on August 1, 1968. Section 1902 stipulated that in implementing the legislation, the California Delinquency Prevention Commission was to cooperate with county Delinquency Prevention Commissions and the Youth Authority on (1) establishing program guidelines and (2) selecting the four programs from locally submitted proposals. The following two paragraphs state the essential standards developed by joint effort of the above mentioned groups:

> The purpose of the Youth Service Bureau Act is to offer an incentive and opportunity for local agencies (both public and private) to pool their resources and develop innovative programs to divert young people from entering into the juvenile justice system. The Youth Service Bureau is a place in the community to which delinquent and delinquent prone youths can be referred by parents, law enforcement agencies, the schools, etc. It should have a wide range of services reflecting the coordination and integration of important public and private prevention resources existing in the community.

> A neighborhood center is envisioned in a location central to the community (or a target area within the community) with day to day operations and services under the

direction of a Youth Services Coordinator. Participating agencies, organizations, and volunteers would contribute full or part-time staff and supportive services for the children and youth served.[16]

The program legislation, guidelines, and standards were disseminated to each county's Delinquency Prevention Commission. Meetings were held in Southern California and in Northern California to review with county Delinquency Prevention Commission representatives, California's diversion and youth service bureau approach. These meetings stimulated interest in developing local proposals. Also, information about diversion and youth service bureaus and the availability of state funds was distributed to various county groups, including chiefs of police, probation officers, sheriffs, County Juvenile Justice Commissions, the Urban League, the NAACP, United Fund Organizations, and local community action groups (League of Women Voters, Lawyers' Wives, and so on). These groups received descriptions of the youth service bureau legislation and the deadlines for submitting proposals for the four pilot youth service bureau projects.[17] Before the four pilot projects were selected, the Youth Authority applied for Law Enforcement Assistance Administration (LEAA) funds from the California Council on Criminal Justice (CCCJ) to help fund additional youth service bureaus. The LEAA application was approved, and the state received a $150,000 federal grant to increase the number of pilot projects from four to nine. The remaining funds were to be used by the Youth Authority's Division of Research and Development to evaluate the projects.

In early February, 1969 the nine pilot projects were selected from a total of twenty-five proposals. The stated selection criteria were: (1) eligibility in accordance with published guidelines and standards, (2) degree of community involvement of both public and private agencies, (3) program content, (4) uniqueness of target area and connection between target area needs and youth service bureau program, and (5) a demonstration that the proposed bureau was not a part of an existing program.

State funding for these pilot projects was discontinued in June, 1971. Eight of the pilot projects subsequently applied directly to CCCJ through a local (city or county) unit of government for refunding for the fiscal year 1971-1972. The local unit provided the required matching funds (approximately 20 percent) through in-kind services. By these means, the counties were able to expand the youth service bureaus funding (now being termed "Special Grant Diversion Units) substantially beyond the previous $25,000 annual level.[18]

In summary, diversion was a federal proposal that in California included provisions for state and federal funds for those local program proposals which met the proposed program guidelines. Local agencies could receive funds in exchange for adopting a particular form of diversion program. Therefore, the incorporation of diversion programs by local agencies can be seen as a predictable response to an external financial opportunity and nationwide reform movement.

North County's Development of Diversion

North County was one of the nine counties selected for a state and federally funded youth service bureau pilot program. The county's Delinquency Prevention Commission encouraged several cities in the county to develop proposals for youth service bureau programs to be entered in the statewide competition. Three cities submitted proposals.

The proposal selected was developed by what was called the "Inter-Agency Committee," which included representatives from a number of local organizations, one of which was the Model Cities Agency. When the proposal was approved, the Delinquency Prevention Commission and Model Cities personnel worked together to select a program coordinator. In addition, several county agency personnel were loaned to the bureau for several hours per week. These included a deputy probation officer, a police officer, an employment counselor, a psychiatrist, and a public health nurse. Two paraprofessionals worked with the bureau full-time. The youth service bureau was in operation for two years and, according to its reports, made contacts with more than 500 youths. Most of these contacts involved assistance in job placement. The bureau was discontinued when the state and federal funds were terminated.

This pilot program provided the basic philosophical and operational framework for North County juvenile court's move into diversion programs. An external financial opportunity facilitated the county juvenile court's interest in diversion; the County Administrator informed the probation officer that a city within North County had received a substantial Model Cities grant, part of whose funds were appropriated for delinquency prevention programs. The probation officer said,

> The Model Cities concept involved the use of citizen task force groups to determine various city needs. One task force was concerned with crime reduction and decided that the prevention of delinquency was a primary need. Therefore, we became involved in attempting to fill this need, through the utilization of Model Cities funds.

86

The Model Cities Agency was familiar with securing federal grants, and this led to a partnership between the Model Cities Agency and the juvenile court. The two organizations combined efforts to develop a federal proposal through CCCJ for two county diversion programs. One program was to deal with the Model Cities target area (the western part of the county), while the second program would serve the central area of the county.[19]

North County juvenile court's move into diversion by securing federal funds was explained by the probation officer as "a fashionable trend of the time in going after federal grants" and a "natural administrative response to available funds." The probation officer elaborated, saying that during the late 1960s, many city and county government agencies (law enforcement, employment, health, social welfare, etc.) looked for federal grants. Beginning in the Johnson administration, federal funds for local social services were increasingly available. This trend was demonstrated by the Omnibus Crime Bill and the Safe Streets Act of 1968 which created the Law Enforcement Assistance Administration (LEAA) in the U. S. Department of Justice. The LEAA required the establishment of a planning agency (the CCCJ in California) in each state to administer the federal bloc grant program for state or local programs meeting federal guidelines oriented toward reducing crime through improving the criminal justice system. Therefore, given the size of federal funds being made available for delinquency control, the county probation officer stated, "It was only natural to go after the funds that would assist us in the expansion of our court services."[20] This statement reflects the probation officer's view of local government agencies as adaptable mechanisms that should be responsive to external opportunities that help fill their needs.

In exchange for federal funds, local agencies developed federally prescribed diversion programs reflecting particular programmatic priorities in favor at the time. According to the director of the county diversion program, shortly after the President's Crime Commission report on crime and delinquency and the congressional appropriation of funds, diversion became "the name of the game for federal funding." As more federal money became available, CCCJ began to give greater priority to proposals submitted by law enforcement, court, and correction agencies that included diversion program orientations. In part, traditional agencies were favored over alternate (i.e., private) agencies because the traditional agencies became more adept at submitting grant proposals, and the funding procedures became more institutionalized. This was the case with the CCCJ's reorganization into what was called a "regional systems approach," in which each regional CCCJ agency determined its own goals and funding priorities within the general state framework and distributed its bloc grant funds accordingly. Previously, all CCCJ grant proposals and decisions had been made at the state level. The regional system approach facilitated a drift from LEAA program and funding goals and guidelines in favor of local concerns and formal agency needs.[21]

IMPLEMENTATION OF
DIVERSION PROGRAMS

North County juvenile court's diversion programs became operational in early 1972. As has been stated the earlier youth service bureaus had been administered jointly by the county Delinquency Prevention Commission and the Model Cities group. The change in name from "youth service bureau" to "diversion programs" was an attempt by the new program director to eliminate any connection between the old and the new programs, a change deemed necessary because of the public perception that the earlier program had not been successful. Nonetheless, the philosophy and goals of the new diversion programs were modeled on those of the earlier program in such areas as delinquency prevention, family crisis intervention, and diversion from the formal juvenile court system. The diversion program included four interrelated program components: a drug abuse prevention unit, an outreach center, a neighborhood youth house, and family intervention units.

Drug Abuse Prevention Unit

The drug abuse prevention unit's primary functions were to educate community groups about various drugs and about rehabilitation and counseling techniques for drug users and the community treatment resources available to drug users. Though able to service both public and private groups, the unit dealt primarily with the juvenile court and the police. Its operations were a part of the diversion program's overall attempt to coordinate community resources into an understandable and usable referral system for various youth-related problems. Its focus on drug-related education and coordination with referral resources was directly related to the availability of funds for drug-related services. The police department of the target population's city received a federal grant part of which was designated for drug abuse prevention and treatment. This part it transferred into the diversion program to provide for the salaries of a full-time program coordinator and a half-time secretary.

The drug abuse prevention unit became fully operational in June 1972. It established a referral system to which individuals in need of assistance with drug problems could be sent for help. North County juvenile court and the diversion program components used the unit to handle cases involving youths they felt were in need of drug treatment referrals, but its primary function, according to the diversion program director, was to train court diversion staff and familiarize them with handling drug problems with the community referral resources available.[22]

Outreach Center

The Outreach Center focused on individual counseling and youth group work and coordinated the efforts of other community agencies offering youth services. The assumption that underlay the center's activities was that delinquency is the result not only of a youth's behavior but of a lack of constructive involvement by community residents and organizations. The center staff included the diversion program director, a program developer, counseling staff (deputy probation officers), clerical workers, and a cadre of Neighborhood Youth Corps students, volunteers, and donated staff from public agencies.[23]

The Outreach Center's services were both direct and indirect. The direct services included individual or group counseling, employment assistance, tutoring services, and what the center termed "cultural enrichment experiences." It also sponsored youth clubs, athletic teams, karate classes, sewing classes, and youth leadership training conferences and served as a drop-in center for youths to play games, or engage in "rap sessions." These activities were "developed in an effort to help the youngster develop a positive self-image and greater interest in relating to others.[24]

Indirect services which the center provided to the general community included helping other community youth serving agencies. The diversion program director stated that the Outreach Center served the community both in an advisory capacity for youth-oriented problems and neighborhood youth projects (e.g., a neighborhood house, a drop-in center) and as a central coordinating agency that could assist community groups in gaining access to various economic, educational, and advisory resources for youth-related services.

A youth's contact with the Outreach Center's program could begin with a referral from an agency, his or her parents, or a self-referral. Youths who referred themselves were usually seeking employment assistance. This could result in a direct referral to a local employment agency. In many instances the result was an interview to help define what one of the counselors called a "realistic job orientation" (e.g., what is this youth qualified for?) with a possible recommendation of further education or specific job training. According to one counselor in the Outreach Center, many of the youths who referred themselves were urged to do so by the police.

The typical law enforcement referral to the center was made through a citation system, which began when the police issued a citation to a youth and sent a copy to the Outreach Center. After receiving the citation, the center staff would make three attempts to contact the youth, by telephone, by letter, and finally by a visit to the youth's home. Following contact and screening, a disposition decision would be reached that might include individual counseling, involvement in center activities, or referral to diversion's family intervention units for family counseling. The most frequent disposition was individual counseling with a caseworker. Verification of the center's contact and disposition of referred youth would then be forwarded to the police. Generally a youth's contact with the center was not to exceed six months, although in many cases contact did extend beyond that period. The diversion program director stated, he required written statements by the caseworkers explaining why they believed a case should be continued beyond six months and in many such cases, allowed the extension.

Neighborhood Youth House

The Youth House was used as an alternative to the county detention facility for youths aged 13 to 18 for stays not to exceed four months. The Youth House could accommodate up to eight girls and boys. Its staff consisted of a full-time director, a half-time secretary, and two houseparents. Residents were referred by their parents, other diversion units, the juvenile court, the police, or were self-referrals. In most instances, the Youth House was used to provide temporary residence for youths whose parents would not allow them to return home at the time or for youths who were likely to experience further problems if they returned home immediately. Normally when a minimal level of reconciliation between the youth and his or her parents was achieved, the youth returned home and the family participated in diversion's family counseling services. Where reconciliation was not achieved, a petition would be filed in the juvenile court and a suitable out-of-home placement would be sought for the youth.[25]

Family Intervention Units

The family intervention units were to provide a direct juvenile court diversion function. The primary targets were "incorrigible" cases, youths whose problems were viewed as family-centered. A court-prepared description of the family intervention units specified the target youth cases:

1. Only cases whose parents or guardians resided in the target city limits.

90

2. All 601 cases admitted to the juvenile hall that were presently not active.

3. All citations for 601s (these cases could involve a minor 602 offense or truancy if it was determined to be incidental to the 601 aspect of the case).

4. Minor 601 cases--i.e., petty theft, malicious mischief, curfew, alcoholic offenses (nontraffic), drug cases (involving possession or use but not selling), burglary by a youth aged 14 years or younger, joyriding and other misdemeanors--admitted to the juvenile hall that were not presently active or had been dismissed for ninety days or longer.

5. No cases of great public notoriety.

6. No offenses involving drug selling, robbery, burglary by a youth 15 years or older, grand theft auto, traffic, or violence or sexual assault.[26]

In effect, the family intervention units offered family counseling services to youths and their families in cases where a youth's incorrigibility, truancy, runaway, or other behavior problem was associated with his or her family. A guiding assumption was that a youth's behavior problems were "relative and proportionate to the transaction and communication among family members and cannot be helped without family participation."[27]

Normally a family would enter the family intervention process following a family crisis involving a youth's behavior. Often the youth was at the juvenile court intake stage and thus separated from the family; perhaps the parents were considering having the youth removed from the home. The caseworker supervisor of one unit explained that in most instances parents would have a child placed in detention for punishment, indicating that they would take formal action if he or she did not meet their behavior expectations in the future. The supervisor contended that although many lower class families attempted to punish their children by turning them over to the police and juvenile court, they would feel guilty about "turning the kid over to the authorities." In these instances, the parents were interested in getting the youths back home, thinking that now they knew their parents would take formal action if their behavior warranted it. So to get their children home, these families would generally agree to family intervention's minimum requirement of participating in five counseling sessions in which the youths, parents, and siblings were to be present.[28]

In cases involving families with a more middle-class pattern, several of the unit staff contended that financial coercion was a common tactic to encourage the parents to participate in family intervention. The basic argument put forth by family intervention staff was that if the youth remained in juvenile hall, a petition would be filed and the youth would probably be returned home after several days. As an end result, the parents would be billed for the youth's stay in detention. In addition, the unit supervisor continued, "we include a lot of propaganda as to the negative behavioral effects a stay in juvenile hall can have on their child." [29]

It should be pointed out that before the family intervention services, a youth's first referral to detention intake on a 601 or minor 602 offense would normally result in an outright release or a release on informal probation without supervision. For example, in 1971, one year before diversion, detention intake statistics of one county area showed 195 of 296 referrals closed at intake. In 1972, diversion's first year, 1 of 266 referrals from this area were closed at intake. This illustrates the probation officer's statement that, "We felt 'diversion' to be a way of implementing good informal probation."[30]

The five required family counseling sessions began with a caseworker's observation of what was going on in the family unit offering remedies for observed problems. The intervention counselor attempted to diagnose the problems and bring them out into the open. Once the family members acknowledged the problem, a more permanent form of therapy was sought through various community referral sources. A frequent referral made by family intervention was probation. According to the casework supervisor, youths referred to probation from family intervention usually received out-of-home placements, namely, in a foster home or in an institution. This suggests that in instances in which families and youths were not able to comply or progress with the diversion program requirements, the youths were generally considered inappropriate for the probation department's regular home supervision. Other referrals included community mental health associations; social services; Home, Health, and Counseling Services (a local agency); the probation department's family service unit; and marital counseling groups. A casework supervisor stated that in all cases involving referrals to other agencies, the caseworker was required to accompany the family as a group or individual members to the first several counseling sessions. Following this, the caseworker maintained contact with the referral agency to monitor the progress of the family or individual members. [31]

92

In summary, the implementation of the diversion program in North County was based on the assumption that by coordinating and using community resources, the problem of delinquency could be dealt with successfully. Delinquency was generally viewed as the primary result of what Lemert terms a "dilapidated social structure," which produces not only troubled individuals but families with multiple problems.[32] The distinction between the youth as an individual and the family unit was not sharply maintained, as can be seen in this description of the way the components of the diversion program were implemented. It is interesting to note that though many writers in the field of delinquency connect the family with delinquent conduct, the connection is based on a statistical rather than causal relationship, which does not separate the influence of the family from other intervening variables such as poverty, slum residence, and lack of education.[33] Nonetheless, during this study North County's family intervention efforts were expanding to ensure the court's capability for what the diversion program director termed "earlier and earlier intervention" into families beginning to experience problems with their children.[34]

The concept of diversion is predicated on the assumption that the formal juvenile court system is destructive and that it is more effective to direct youths into less stigmatizing programs. However, what emerges in this study is that diversion in practice becomes an extension of the court's control over youths and their families. The thrust of diversion's family intervention and earlier detection of families with problem youths, therefore, appears to be contrary to the conceptual rationale of diversion. In effect, North County's diversion practices focused on many youths who would not previously have been subject to court control, in order to prevent their possible misconduct in the future.

IMPACT OF THE DIVERSION PROGRAMS

In Table 5.1 (second page following), arrest and court handling comparisons are made between the percentages in 1972 (diversion's first year of operation) and the mean percentages for 1969 to 1971. These comparisons appear consistent with the official goal of diversion as expressed by the President's Crime Commission: to divert youths from the formal juvenile court process. The 1972 arrests, juvenile intake referrals, and cases receiving juvenile court petitions each indicate declines in percentage from the 1969-1971 mean percentages. The declines are probably related to the existence of the diversion program. In 1972, the police were able to refer selected youths to the diversion program instead of arresting and referring them to juvenile court intake. Fewer arrests and court intake referrals together with more cases closed at intake or placed under informal probation account for the decreased number of juvenile court petitions. Diversion provides court intake staff with an alternative to traditional juvenile court processing and results in fewer juvenile court petitions filed.

In 1972, the diversion units received a total of 1,691 referrals originating from the juvenile court, police, parents, schools, and youths themselves (self-referrals). Only 9 of the total 1,691 referrals were closed at intake. Of the 1,682 diversion clients, 1,179 received family intervention service, 54 resided at the Youth House, and 449 were handled by the Outreach Center. The disproportionate number of youths receiving family services is attributable to the presence of a large number of indirect referrals of siblings. The presence of parents and all siblings in the family was required in the family intervention process.

The summary totals of youths under some form of court and diversion control from 1969 to 1972 are presented in Table 5.2 (second page following). Included are the proportions of North County's youth population under control. Differentiation is made between direct and indirect sibling referrals. Between 1971 and 1972, the number of youths under some form of control increased by 823; this is an increase from 0.03 to 0.04 when compared to all youths in the jurisdiction. The portion of youths directly referred and under control remained constant in 1972 as in the previous years, but when the indirect sibling referrals are included, the proportion increases substantially.

Table 5.3 (third page following) measures the change in the number of youths under control as a result of diversion. A transitional probability was used to compute an expected number of youths to be under control in 1972. A comparison of the expected number with actual numbers, differentiated again on the basis of direct and indirect sibling referral estimates, resulted in an increase from 2.4 percent to 32.1 percent. If it were available, a measure of time youths spend under control would be useful, since the "amount of control" is a function of both the number of youths under control and the amount of time they spend under control. Additionally, since the family intervention service is not limited to directly referred youths and their siblings but includes the parents as well, the net-widening presented here is an underestimate because the parents have not been included in numerical totals for family intervention.

Table 5.1

Youth Population, Arrests, Court
Referral, and Subsequent Disposition

| | MEAN | |
	1969-1971	1972
Youthful population, age 10-17	86,910	88,316
Juvenile arrests	14,348	12,447
Percent of youthful population	16.5	14.1
Juvenile court intake referrals	5,612	4,661
Percent of youthful population	6.5	5.3
Referrals closed at intake or placed under informal probation	3,428	3,201
Percent of intake referrals	61.1	68.7
Petitions filed in juvenile court	2,184	1,460
Percent of intake referrals	38.9	31.1

Table 5.2

Summary Totals of Youths Under Some Form of Juvenile Court
or Diversion Control as a Result of Direct
Referrals and Indirect Sibling Referrals to
Family Intervention

	1969	1970	1971	1972
Directly referred youths receiving informal, formal, or diversion control	2,755	2,285	2,676	2,713
Indirect sibling referrals to family intervention control	----	----	----	786
Total number of youths under some form of probation or diversion control	2,755	2,285	2676	3499
Proportion of county youth population under control	0.03	0.03	0.03	0.04

Table 5.3

Comparison of the Expected Number of Youths
Under Control in 1972 with Actual Number of
Youths Under Control Including a Two-Sibling
Estimate [35]

	Number of Youths Expected to be under Control	Difference	Percentage Increase
Actual number of youths under control----2,713	2,649	+ 64	2.4
Actual number of youths under control, including a two-sibling estimate----3,499	2,649	+ 850	32.1

It is significant to note that of the 1,179 youths involved in the family intervention service, 88 ultimately received juvenile court petitions requesting suitable out-of-home placements. These 88 youths were referred to the juvenile court because their families were unable or unwilling to comply with the family intervention methods. The family intervention staff reasoned that if families did not respond to the family-centered treatment, the child (and siblings) should be removed from the home. Failure to comply or to progress with family treatment was felt to indicate family disorganization. Essentially, families found not to be amenable to family intervention were viewed as having limited potential for providing the appropriate child socialization necessary to prevent future troublesome behavior.

An important issue that emerges from these findings relates to diversion's role in depressing, creating, or even accelerating delinquency. In part this reflects the concerns that have grown out of the labeling theory literature. As reviewed in Chapter 1, labeling theorists have argued that formal interaction with social control agencies is an important component involved in the perpetuation of delinquency. While the data from the present study are not intended to address this issue, several pertinent implications have emerged. Specifically, these findings have shown that diversion produces net-widening, measured by larger numbers of youths receiving some form of juvenile court service or control, as well as accelerated control, determined on the basis of out-of-home placement of youths whose families are unable or unwilling to comply with family intervention. In the latter instance, what often happens is that siblings with no prior behavior problems are accelerated into the formal court system for what is termed a "suitable out-of-home placement," which can include placement with relatives or in foster homes, group homes, or institutions. The potential of this practice to accelerate youth behavior problems or actually to create delinquency is a major concern that will be elaborated upon in Chapter 7.

In summary, diversion influenced North County juvenile court's youth handling practices in two ways. First, the program initiated an intentional displacement process (intended consequence) whereby youths who earlier would have been considered suitable for existing court services and forms of control are judged in this less constraining decision-making framework to be suitable for diversion. A second, unintended consequence of the program was that youths (and therefore their parents as well) who would not previously have been considered for court service and control at all, are judged suitable for diversion. Together these findings indicated that diversion's official purpose, limiting the jurisdiction of the juvenile court, has not been achieved. Instead, diversion has enlarged the scope of the juvenile court and the proportion of the population under its control, resulting in a form of net-widening that substantially exceeds the net-widening effects of the Boys' Center and probation subsidy.

Several important and alarming questions emerge from this study's findings about net-widening. Overall, the findings reflect the growth of the state via the juvenile court system. This growth is particularly evident in the efforts and results of diversion's family intervention activities. Chapter 6 considers the question of whether net-widening and the associated growth of the state foreshadows the "coming of a minimum security society" within the U. S. in which state jurisdiction and social control powers will be expanded.

1. Rosenheim, M. "Youth Service Bureaus: A Concept in Search of Definition." Juvenile Court Judges Journal 20 (1969):69.

2. For discussion see President's Commission on Law Enforcement and Administration of Justice Task Force Report: Juvenile Delinquency and Youth Crime. U. S. Government Printing Office, 1967 and Sheridan, W. H. "Juveniles Who Commit Noncriminal Acts: Why Treat in a Correction System?" Federal Probation 31 (1967):26-36.

3. President's Commission Task Force Report, p. 8.

4. President's Commission Task Force Report, p. 8.

5. President's Commission Task Force Report, p. 8.

6. President's Commission Task Force Report, p. 8.

7. President's Commission Task Force Report, p. 9.

8. President's Commission Task Force Report, p. 9.

9. President's Commission on Law Enforcement and Administration of Justice Task Force Report: The Challenge of Crime in a Free Society. U. S. Government Printing Office, 1967, p. 83.

10. President's Commission Task Force Report: Juvenile Delinquency and Youth Crime, p. 20.

11. Rosenheim, p. 70.

12. For discussion on middle-class family access to alternative resources for youth problems, see Cicourel, A. The Social Organization of Juvenile Justice. John Wiley and Sons, Inc., 1968, pp. 273-291.

13. For discussion of the various youth service bureau program models that have evolved, see Norman, S. The Youth Service Bureau: A Brief Description with Five Current Programs. National Council on Crime and Delinquency, 1970, pp. 5-6.

14. Underwood, W. A. "California's Youth Service Bureaus" Youth Authority Quarterly Winter (1969):28.

15. Canlis, M. W. "Tomorrow is Too Late" Youth Authority Quarterly Spring (1968):10.

16. Youth Service Bureaus, Standards and Guidelines. California Delinquency Prevention Commission, October, 1968.

17. Underwood, p. 31.

18. Underwood, pp. 31-32.

19. Interview with North County probation officer.

20. Interview with North County probation officer.

21. Interview with California Youth Authority assistant director for research and development.

22. Interview with North County's diversion program director.

23. Interviews with North County's diversion program director and counseling staff (deputy probation officers) of diversion's Outreach Center.

24. Interviews with counseling staff of diversion's Outreach Center.

25. Interview with North County's director of diversion's Youth House.

26. North County Annual Probation Report, 1972.

27. Satir, V. Conjoint Family Therapy. Science and Behavior Books, Inc., 1967, p. 44.

28. Interview with a North County casework supervisor for a diversion family intervention unit.

29. Interview with casework supervisor for a diversion family intervention unit.

30. North County Annual Probation Report, 1971; North County Annual Probation Report, 1972; and interview with North County probation officer.

31. Interviews with the casework supervisor and staff of a diversion family intervention unit.

32. Lemert, E. Instead of Court: Diversion in Juvenile Justice. U. S. Government Printing Office, 1971, p. 71.

33. For discussion, see Blomberg, T. G. and S. L. Caraballo "Accelerated Family Intervention in Juvenile Justice: An Exploration and a Recommendation for Constraint" Crime and Delinquency October (1979):497-502.

34. Interview with North County's diversion program director.

35. To compute the expected number of youths to be under some form of control during diversion's first year of operation--a transitional probability was used. In this case, the transitional probability is a mean of the proportion of county youth population under control during 1969-1971. The expected number of youths to be under control was computed by multiplying the transitional probability or .03 by the 1972 youth population of 88,316. Additionally, an estimated number of youths to be subject to control is provided which includes the two sibling estimate reported by family intervention staff of the 393 youths directly referred to diversion's family intervention program.

CHAPTER 6

NET-WIDENING AND THE COMING
OF A MINIMUM SECURITY SOCIETY

JUVENILE COURT ORGANIZATIONS
AND REFORMS

Two major purposes of this study were (1) to describe North County's experiences with and implementation of three community correction reform programs and (2) to document the net-widening impact of the court's implementation of these reforms. In assessing the developmental background of the Boys' Center, probation subsidy, and diversion, it was shown that a concern for organizational stability and related financial stability was a major motive underlying North County's development of these professional youth services. Following the inception of each program the reform was intentionally implemented as a supplement to court practice. In each case this resulted in a modification of the court's administration of services to youths and eventuated in net-widening.

An essential question that emerges from these findings is how major reform programs come to be implemented into juvenile court policy in ways contrary or directly opposite to their conceptual rationales. This question concerns the organizational transformation of reforms and makes it necessary to consider the organization of juvenile court. Several characteristics of this organization were identified in this study's formulation of a perspective on juvenile court organization. These characteristics suggest that the court will respond to those program opportunities which it perceived as compatible with the functional necessities, goals, and practices of its organization. The reasons for this is that the court operates under conditions of conflicting goals, ambiguous treatment technology, scarcity of resources, and operational uncertainty. Additionally, ever-present operational uncertainty predisposes the court to implement reform programs which will supplement previous formal or informal court practices instead of significantly altering court practices. In the instances of the Boys' Center, probation subsidy, and diversion, the court was able to tailor each program to what it perceived to be in the best interests of its court organization and therefore in the best interest of its youthful clients. Thus, given the character of the juvenile court organization, the transformation of these community correction reforms from apparently liberating concepts to mechanisms for accelerated youth control was a predictable outcome.

The Boys' Center, probation subsidy, and diversion can be understood as parts of a larger movement to alter the nature of the juvenile court. A major index of this alteration is the difference over time in the distribution of court services meted out to youths and more recently, in the case of diversion, to their families. In the last two decades, it has been demonstrated that court services have shifted from conducting social case histories and informal and formal home supervision for youths on probation to providing a local correctional establishment complete with diagnostic facilities, intensive home supervision, family intervention services, institutional facilities, parole services, and miscellaneous mechanisms for substantial community information gathering and surveillance. These increases in local court services have largely resulted from conscious state and federal policies that have reduced local autonomy because of increased local dependence on centralized funds.

THE EXTENT OF
NET-WIDENING

The change in character of the juvenile court has corresponded with increasing coordination among local, state, and federal correction agencies, not only in the case of youths but adult offenders as well. The nationwide explosion of community correction reforms at the local level for both youthful and adult offenders has not led to a decline in the number or population of state and federal correction institutions as officially intended. In fact, the Bureau of Justice statistics show that in 1981, despite a stable base population, the number of people in state and federal prisons increased by a record 12.1 percent. The Bureau reported that for every 100,000 Americans there are 154 inmates. During 1981, federal prisons operated at 17 percent above their inmate capacities. In the states of Alabama, Alaska, Utah, Hawaii, Washington, Idaho, North Dakota, Maryland, and Indiana, the prison population increased by 20 percent. Moreover, the number of states under a federal court order to reduce overcrowding rose from 28 to 31. The number of states involved in lawsuits over prison conditions increased from 32 to 37. In addition, 1,009 men and women were awaiting execution in 31 of the 36 states that allows capital punishment. This reflects a 100 percent increase in the intervening three years. When the approximately 150,000 adults held in local jails and 60,000 youths in state and local facilities are considered, the cumulative figure reveals that approximately 2 million people are locked up or under official supervision on any given day in the U.S.[1] These figures would more than double if consideration were given to the increasing number of family members encouraged or required to submit to various family intervention services because a family member is either in trouble with or likely to get into trouble with the law.[2]

Beyond the substantial client growth of the criminal and juvenile justice systems, substantial client net-widening is occurring within the mental health system. For example, one of the first acts of the 1977 President's Commission on Mental Health was to increase by 50 percent the number of people considered to have mental problems. The Commission reported that information then current revealed that 15 percent of the American population, namely 20 to 32 million people, were in need of some form of mental health service. These figures did not include school age children, an estimated 15 percent of whom were in need of services for various psychological disorders or an estimated half million Americans dependent on heroin, 10 million with alcohol related difficulties, the elderly, etc.[3]

Messinger has argued that social control practices and trends in the modern United States signal the coming of a minimum security society in which an ever increasing proportion of the base population will become subject to some form of control.[4] However, while increases in future social control do appear likely, it is unclear whether or not all such social control efforts are unnecessary, futile, self-serving, and without individual and social benefits.

NET-WIDENING AND ASSOCIATED
POLICY IMPLICATIONS

It is important to recognize that there are different opinions about whether net-widening is good or bad. For example, there is substantial support for more extensive crime and behavior control measures, measures which would eventuate in accelerated net-widening. In part this position reflects the notion of agents of the justice system and of other formal systems that the more control and/or service they administer, the greater is the likelihood that they can reduce various social problems. In contrast, there are recommendations for a "hands-off" or "non-intervention" approach to certain crimes and other behavioral difficulties.[5] This position reflects concern over the negative labeling and damaging delinquent or criminal associations that are presumed to be connected with contacts with the official system or alternative programs. There is also a position that can be termed "equivocal or ambivalent."[6] This orientation includes simultaneous concerns over the negative client effects of net-widening and violations of freedom, and concern about the need for various forms of state intervention and their potential usefulness in relieving human misery and reducing social problems.

While it is unclear where youth corrections will go in the future, it is a safe guess that the "hands-off" or "non-intervention" approach will not be prominent. Current trends do suggest that in the future some form of control will be exercised over a larger and less seriously troubled sector of the youth population and their families. The possibility of such a trend indicates the need for responsible evaluation which specifies the various results, expected and unexpected, of these efforts. There will be a need in future correction policy for differentiations of the potential for positive and negative results in various programs. What is being suggested here is that while it is insufficient to document only expected outcomes, it is equally insufficient to document only unexpected outcomes. Instead, what are now needed to guide responsible youth correction policies are multi-goal evaluation studies concerned simultaneously with the intended, the unintended, and positive and negative outcome potentials of various reform efforts and with the specific program processes that produce these various outcomes for different client groups. Multi-goal evaluation studies are largely nonexistent. However, it should be possible to carry out such studies on implementations of various correction reforms to examine what certain programs and service processes can and cannot do, thereby providing a basis for informed correctional policies.

NOTES

1. U.P.I. "U.S. Prison Rolls Soar by Record 12 Percent." New York Times, May 12, 1982 and A.P. "Rise in Prisons' Populations Attributed to Tougher Laws." New York Times, May 2, 1982.

2. Messinger, S. L. "Punishments' Troubling Future." Chicago Tribune, December 16, 1977.

3. President's Commission on Mental Health Vol. I. U.S. Government Printing Office, 1978, pp. 4, 8, and 9.

4. Messinger, S. L. Personal correspondence, 1980.

5. For discussion see Schur, E. M. Radical Non-Intervention: Rethinking the Delinquency Problem. Prentice-Hall, Inc., 1973.

6. For discussion see Klein, M. and K. Teilmann (eds.). Handbook of Criminal Justice Evaluation. Sage Publishing Company, 1980, pp. 9-17.

CHAPTER 7

THE RESULTS OF DIVERSION

During the past several years, the evaluation literature concerning various effects of diversion programs has grown substantially. Though the results reported in this literature are not even or conclusive, several significant trends have appeared. First, while no specific diversion program has been found optimal for all or even most diversion clients, certain diversion programs appear to be effective with various combinations of youths. Second, and consistent with the results of this study, it has been demonstrated that diversion programs are capable of producing "net-widening," extending the client reach of the juvenile court system by selecting a major portion of their clients from groups not previously subject to court processing. Third, diversion programs have been shown to produce a number of detrimental consequences both for youths and their families, including increased rearrest rates, unwanted intrusions into the family, and accelerated insertion into the court system for clients not amenable to diversion programs.

Several recent publications on diversion have focused on explaining the disparate results of diversion programs. For example, Klein contends that the net-widening and related detrimental consequences for clients of diversion does not demonstrate failure of the diversion concept, but instead reflects failure in the program implementation of the concept.[1] Lemert elaborates that diversion's net-widening results can be largely attributed to the cooptation of diversion by law enforcement agencies, partly because of their dominant and narrowly conceived social control function.[2] Austin and Krisberg contend that diversion has contributed to "wider, stronger, and different nets" of control because of a functioning of organizational dynamics which have resisted, distorted, and frustrated diversion's original purposes.[3]

Moreover, Polk asserts that despite a disparate result record, diversion is a "hardy practice" capable of surviving in modified form for many years to come.[4] Polk supports his assertion by discussing possible future increases in the numbers of troubled youths, and the widespread concern about doing something for them.

Overall, the characteristics of diversion--its developmental background, its implementation, and the currently incomplete understanding we have of it--are typical of other community correction reforms, including local institutions and intensive community supervision programs. Though it is unclear what these programs can and cannot do for youths of various types, many of them continue to operate nonetheless. Indeed, diversion proliferates despite its ever-present potential for negative as well as positive results. Clearly there is a pressing need for the relative value of these programs to be specified in order for correction program policies to be guided responsibly. This chapter addresses this need by reviewing the evaluation literature of diversion with the purpose of identifying an evaluation approach capable of producing findings that address the question of what diversion and other correction programs can and cannot do for clients of various types.

EVALUATION RESULTS
OF DIVERSION

With few exceptions, evaluation studies of diversion programs have tended to fall into one of two categories, documenting either diversion's positive or its negative results. To date, there has been a notable absence of diversion literature in the area of multi-goal evaluation studies concerned with both what specific diversion programs and/or services can do and cannot do for particular clients.

Positive Results

Diversion was originally proposed as a more effective approach to delinquency control than the traditional juvenile court system approach. Often, in assessing diversion's effectiveness, studies have focused on measuring the subsequent delinquency of diversion's clients and comparing it to that of clients who have been handled traditionally. For example, a study of several California counties shows that Duxbury reported lower juvenile arrests during the operation of diversion programs than when the programs were not in operation. [5] In the evaluation reports by Baron et al., Thornton et al., Forward et al., Klein, Ku and Blew, and Quay and Love, lower rearrest rates were reported for diversion clients as compared with similar cases handled by the juvenile court. [6] Klein's study employed random assignment of youths to diversion and non-diversion program conditions and found that diverted youths (i.e., diversion without services) had a significantly lower recidivism rate than youths who were the subjects of juvenile court petitions.

California's diversion evaluation study referred to in Chapter 5 has assessed a number of diversion programs that were initiated in 1974 by the California Youth Authority. [7] Several recent publications have reported various results from this evaluation study. While the published results have not revealed consistent findings across programs, a number of interesting program-specific results have been reported. For example,

Bohnstedt reports that three diversion programs did reduce client recidivism to an extent that was statistically and practically significant.[8] These results were based upon comparisons of diversion program clients matched with comparison cases handled by the juvenile court. Two of the three programs relied upon family intervention treatment strategies in their delivery of client services.

Palmer and Lewis reported on the final phase of the evaluation of California Youth Authority diversion. Relying on findings from a quasi-experimental design, the authors argue that youths of some types might benefit most from short-term, voluntary diversion programs operated by non-justice-system personnel. Other types of youths might be best served by longer term, non-voluntary diversion programs staffed by justice personnel. Youths of other types might benefit most from some variation of these two diversion program orientations and still others from outright release with no diversion program service whatsoever. The authors argue for outright release only if no violent offenses has been committed and more generally, urge that diversion program intervention occur not before the second offense and no later than the third offense.[9]

The State of Florida has published the evaluation results of a three-site pilot project designed to divert youth offenders from the juvenile court. Through a contract award procedure, local non-profit organizations received contracts either to provide or to arrange services for diverted youths. The services provided by the three sites included referral to community arbitration boards, work restitution, assignment to volunteers, family counseling, community work service, and employment. After one year of project operation, the three-site evaluation findings revealed 350 monthly client referrals that tended to be white, 15 year-old males with no prior record who had committed misdemeanor property offenses. The average length of project participation for the referrals was 60 days, and the services most commonly received were restitution and community work service. A 9-month follow-up of the youths who participated in the projects and of comparable youths who did not participate indicated a 19 percent rearrest rate for project clients and 24 percent rearrest rate for the comparison group. No significant difference was found between the project and the comparison cases with regard to the seriousness of the subsequent offense.[10]

Net-Widening Results

The fact that diversion is producing net-widening means the programs are producing results exactly opposite to their originally intended purpose, reducing the number of youths who come into contact with the juvenile court. Diversion practices are largely being applied to youths not previously subject to insertion into the juvenile court rather than serving to divert youths previously subject to insertion into the juvenile court into appropriate informal treatment settings.

The empirical literature documenting this net-widening effect of diversion has grown considerably in recent years. Some of the studies comprising this literature include: Austin, Krisberg, and Lawrence; Blomberg; the California Youth Authority; Elliot; Klein; Klein and Tielman; Kutchins and Kutchins; Mattingly and Katkin; Polk; Sarri; and the State of Florida.[11] The data employed in these studies to document net-widening have been either official aggregate statistics or client characteristic profiles.

For example, the California Youth Authority evaluated a number of local diversion projects with a major goal of determining whether or not the projects did indeed divert youths from the traditional juvenile justice system. Two client-type profiles were developed in the evaluation, for "diversion clients" and "prevention clients." Diversion clients were defined as those with the characteristics of youths who would have been processed further into the juvenile justice system if the diversion programs had not been available. Prevention clients were defined as those with the characteristics of youths who would not have been subject to imminent justice system processing in the absence of diversion but were provided diversion program services to prevent future misconduct. Findings reported from eight diversion projects indicated that on the average, less than 50 percent of the program clients were "diversion clients" and the remaining majority were "prevention clients."[12] In a similar study, Klein and Teilman found that youths referred to diversion programs from two southern California police departments tended to be younger, non-serious, non-repeat offenders who prior to diversion would have been released outright. Consequently, the type and number of youths referred to juvenile court was not changed by the operation of the diversion programs.[13]

Studies using official aggregate data in their investigation of diversion's net-widening have used the data to generate what have been termed "transitional probabilities" or "system processing rates." As reviewed earlier, the probabilities or rates are derived from the numerical flow of youths through the juvenile court system of a given jurisdiction for a period of several years before the operation of diversion. Once the probabilities are determined, evaluators are able to project the numbers of youths who would normally come into contact with various components of the juvenile court system (i.e., police, juvenile court intake, juvenile court petition, etc.). Subsequent comparison of these projections with actual numbers of youths coming into contact with the justice system during the operation of diversion programs provides a measurement of the extent of diversion or of net-widening, whichever the case may be. [14]

As a result of these consistent findings of system net-widening together with the previous review of positive client results, it is clear that diversion has a mixed impact. Furthermore the evidence of diversion's net-widening has included documentation of a series of associated detrimental client effects.

Detrimental Client Effects
Associated with Net-Widening

Several studies have reported the association of diversion's net-widening effect with a number of detrimental client effects, which include increased client jeopardy, unwanted intrusions into the family, family disintegration, accelerated insertion into the formal juvenile justice system, and increased behavior difficulties. Klein and Fishman have each documented that mere contact with diversion, particularly for youths affected by net-widening, can increase behavior difficulties because of the increased visibility of youths to diversion "treators" rather than because of increased rates of misconduct. [15]

With regard to increased jeopardy and accelerated insertion into the justice system brought on by diversion, the present study found that when families were unable or unwilling to comply with various diversion program requirements, the children of these families were often removed from the home to receive suitable out-of-home placement by the juvenile court. Further, Polk documented that

> as a direct result of an investigation into the family background of a client referred to the supposed diversion agency, YSB (diversion) staff arranged not only for the direct referral of several other siblings to the Division of Youth Services for direct institutional placement for delinquent tendencies (as well as the client originally referred), but arrest of the mother and father as well for the innovatively invented charge of moral neglect [16]

Obviously, the placement of diversion youths and siblings into institutions presents a number of further dangers as well. [17]

These studies demonstrate that many democratic rights are imperiled by diversion's widening of the client net which stimulates a number of detrimental results. However, as the preceding review documents, these are not the only results of diversion programs. There is some evidence that they can produce beneficial results for youths. Unfortunately, which diversion programs or diversion program services are most useful or most harmful and for whom has yet to be specified.

MULTI-GOAL EVALUATION APPROACH

Characteristic evaluation of diversion and other correction programs has been impeded by what Deutscher terms the "goal trap."[18] The goal trap has influenced previous evaluations of diversion and related correction programs in one of two ways, by facilitating a contrasting focus upon assessments of program goal achievement or by program goal displacement. As documented in this review of diversion, there have been two disparate categories of evaluation findings reported. Assessments of the relative weights of these results vary, but there has been little debate over whether more comprehensive evaluation studies are needed.

In sum, because of the narrow focus which has characterized previous diversion evaluations, it is not yet possible to make meaningful differentiations between the positive and negative results within or across diversion programs. Nonetheless, given the range of diversion program service modalities with their multiplicity of settings, personnel, and client groups, it should be expected that the results of the many different programs that have been implemented would be varied to say the least, and it is possible that what works for various client groups within a program would be different as well.

The importance of the question of what works for whom was recognized by the National Evaluation of the Deinstitutionalization of Status Offenders Program (DSO).[19] The research team employed a comparative framework to assess which project components operating in various community contexts worked best in influencing the behaviors of various groups of status offenders. Included in the study design were assessments of the impact of the program on local juvenile justice systems and related social service agencies, the impact of the flow of cases through the juvenile justice system, and the impact on the local public and key decision-makers.

In several respects, the DSO evaluation approach reflects what Chen and Rossi have termed the "multi-goal theory driven approach" to program evaluation aimed at specifying what a program can and cannot do.[20] Chen and Rossi contend that with few exceptions, program evaluations follow a pattern in which they pick variables from the official proposed program goals that have narrowly defined measurable effects or outcomes and then assess whether or not the program treatments effect those narrowly

112

defined outcomes. If a treatment achieves the effects, the program is considered a success, if not, a failure. The most frequent the findings of evaluation efforts of this type are that the programs did not work. Chen and Rossi claim that the problems associated with conventional evaluation will not be corrected by more rigorous research designs, since such designs would be even less likely to find meaningful program effects. They base their argument on the propositions that: (1) social reform programs are not ordinarily based on a social science understanding of social problems; and (2) program goals determined by administrators and policy-makers are not the results likely to be produced by the programs.[21]

Since the multi-goal evaluation approach promises to generate a much more comprehensive picture of a program's operations, it is likely that program administrators and policy-makers would support it. The cumulative results of such evaluation efforts should provide information pertinent both to the targeted social problem and to effective treatments for the problem. Underlying Chen and Rossi's approach is the assumption that the less that is known about a social problem and how a treatment works, the greater the need for a range of evaluation outcome variables.

Clearly, evaluation studies characteristic of those done in the area of diversion demonstrate narrow orientations toward outcome variables. Moreover, most evaluations of correction programs have not been guided by a concern for the program implementation and the processes which have produced either the positive or negative effects the evaluation finds. The following discussion provides a basic conceptual framework for evaluators who are interested in assessing a broader range of outcome variables of diversion programs or related correction programs and in assessing the program processes which produce these outcome variables for various client groups. The proposed multi-goal framework should be understood as a means of conceptually and substantively integrating the foci and methods of previous evaluations, which have produced diversion's disparate result record.

The approach comprises three interrelated components: client types, services or treatment received, and expected and unexpected outcomes. With few exceptions, previous diversion evaluations have given little attention to describing and differentiating the types of clients handled by diversion programs. Most often diversion program clients have been viewed as a homogeneous aggregate. The major exceptions to this have been evaluation studies concerned with net-widening. These studies have differentiated between system-insertable clients, or intended diversion clients, and non-system-insertable clients, or net-widening clients. It is interesting to note that Palmer and Lewis, in their diversion program evaluation, concluded that various combinations of youths did benefit differently from various diversion program services.[22] Unfortunately, Palmer and Lewis did not specify the characteristics of the youths comprising these combinations of youths who proved appropriate for diversion program services or the particular programs appropriate to those combinations. Certainly, such client type groupings run the risk of imposition in that no client grouping can capture the array of individual client differences or overlap. Nonetheless, groupings of types of clients affected are necessary if evaluators are to provide more comprehensive descriptions of the operations of diversion programs. Furthermore it is likely that evaluators will find that most diversion programs operate with informal or unspoken definitions of client groupings which correspond to their own services and/or handling. While it is unlikely that a common diversion program client typology can be articulated, consideration should be given to such characteristics as age, gender, social class, ethnicity, parental status, school status, area of residence, offense types or reason for referrals (i.e., miscellaneous delinquent behavior, status offender, chemical abuser, etc.), and prior offense histories. Further, initially identified client groupings should be validated through review with diversion program staff.

The next task would be to specify the characteristic ways in which identified client groups are handled. What service or group of services do these groups receive? Who provides services? What is the professional level of the service staff (e.g., voluntary staff, justice staff, social workers, learned professional)? Is participation in the program services voluntary, coerced, or legally mandated? How long do clients receive the service(s)? What action is taken if a client's progress is not satisfactory? How is client progress determined? What form of follow-up service (if any) is provided? In effect, the evaluator must collect various items of information which, taken together, accurately portray the process by which the diversion program delivers services to specific client groups.

The next step is to assess program outcomes pertinent to specific groups and program processes. If Chen and Rossi's recommendation is to be followed, both expected and unexpected outcome variables need to be considered in the outcome assessment. Rearrests or additional referrals for service would be considered, the evaluator should seek unofficial outcomes as well. Client self-reports concerning attitude or changes in self-perception, undetected misconduct, changes in school performance, changes in family relationships, etc., could be included; to this end responses should be sought from youths, teachers, and parents. Unexpected or detrimental outcomes such as net-widening, increased rearrests, negative changes in self-perception or attitude, accelerated entry into the justice system resulting from difficulties with diversion programs and family disintegration should be included in the outcome assessment. However, it is important for evaluators to recognize that mere documentation of net-widening is insufficient. What is needed instead is as comprehensive a specification as possible of the client characteristics and program conditions under which net-widening is either harmful or beneficial. If an unintended client group (i.e., clients who result from net-widening) is drawn into a diversion program and receives services that appear to contribute to keeping them in school, improving their school performance, or helping them gain employment, that needs to be documented. If, on the other hand, unintended client groups are drawn into a diversion program and receive family intervention services that cause family difficulties, those findings have obviously important implications for diversion policy.

In summary, evaluators of diversion and related correction programs should aim their efforts at telling the stories of the programs. Who are their various client groups? How do the programs tend to process their client groups? What are the various positive and negative outcomes for clients, families, and systems that can reasonably be associated with particular client groups and/or program processes? If evaluations are focused on client groups and processes and corresponding outcomes, the goal of producing comprehensive program descriptions, compelling program explanations, and informed program policies become attainable. In effect, the task of evaluation is to probe the cause and effect relationships of program processes and outcomes as they relate to specific client groups. If they do this, evaluators will be in a position to make direct assessments of the relative value of correction programs and reform efforts.

SUMMARY AND CONCLUDING
COMMENTS

It may ultimately be determined that in the case of most youth correction reforms the claim that "nothing works," while an exaggeration, is only a minor one. Or it may be determined on the basis of more broadly conceived evaluation studies that certain reforms and/or services do "work" for some youths but not for others. Presently, given the incomplete empirical understanding of community correction reforms, neither claim is justified.

While multi-goal evaluation of various correction reform programs should clarify what individual programs can and cannot do and for what client groups, a number of other important questions will remain. One major policy question, for example, centers around what the correctional system is and what its purposes are. Another such question is what criteria (e.g., legal, ethical, empirical) must be met before the correction system can legitimately intervene and assume formal or informal jurisdiction over the lives of citizens. Yet another concerns when "coerced treatment" by the correction system is legitimate. Multi-goal evaluation cannot answer these questions, but hopefully the results of such evaluations will play a more important role in future correction policy decisions of which these questions are an integral part.

This study has demonstrated that what is occurring now is an erosion of the distinction between who is in the correction system and who is out of the system but receiving "alternative" control in what was referred to in Chapter 6 as "the coming of a 'minimum security society'." Moreover, the correction system is not only intervening in the lives of an increasingly large proportion of citizens but is frequently doing so without regard for the legal rights of these citizens and without conclusive evidence of a legitimate reason for intervention. But, as evidenced by diversion's record of disparate results (both positive and negative), this 1984 scenario is only one part, although an important part, of the total picture of correction and social control in America today. Another important part of this picture is that in some instances correction intervention is producing positive results. The questions are where to direct correction policy in the future and how to do that?

Repeatedly in the history of correction reform a new philosophical orientation will appear, followed by new associated policies which are characterized by oversold promises. The subsequent failure of these policies to fulfill their promises has led to confusion, cynicism, and frequently to misguided calls for something different. Today, for example, the broad support for community correction is beginning to decline. Alternative recommendations and policies reflect what is being referred to as "a call for an end to the permissive society." These alternatives have included reinstitution of the death penalty, mandatory jail sentences for drunk drivers, longer and mandatory prison sentences, and referral of many young offenders to adult criminal courts. Parents across the nation are joining various self-help programs such as "Toughlove," which emphasizes firmness and discipline to deal with problem children and restore "tolerable" family relationships. Further, many community groups have organized to wage war on drugs, crime, and other local social problems.[23] Associated with these various "get-tough" strategies have been several court decisions which have strengthened local, state, and federal law enforcement capabilities in dealing with criminal suspects. Angry reaction to the Hinckley verdict has stimulated a movement aimed at passage of federal legislation to allow defendants judged insane at the time of their crimes to be punished for those crimes regardless of their mental conditions.[24] In Florida at a news conference a candidate for the Republican party's nomination for the U.S. Senate urged the death penalty for hard-drug smugglers and Turkish-style prisons for all drug violators. [25]

Present social, political, and economical events and the social problems and reactions they reflect are part of a changing society in which various forms of state intervention are becoming increasingly inevitable and necessary. It does appear that both net-widening and this country's recurrent pattern of ever-new reforms in response to crime and other social problems will continue, and with them the ever-present potential for mixed results. Hopefully, policies based upon political propaganda, misconceptions, and/or ignorance about the operation and effects of previous policies will decline in the future. The reaction to the Hinckley verdict, for example, and the controversy that followed, was fueled by substantial and slanted media coverage. The facts that the insanity defense is seldom used and seldom successful and that it is viewed by a number of legal experts as the worst defense a defendant can raise because juries tend to be skeptical of it have not been reported. [26] Recent coverage has also ignored the fact that many defendants who have used insanity defenses successfully have ended up spending more time in mental hospitals than they would have spent in prison for conviction of the same offense. [27] Clearly, policy grounded in the political reaction to the Hinckley verdict would be not only misguided but capable of producing results contrary to the principles and best interests of this society.

With the ever-increasing "fiscal crisis" facing society today and the growing public demand for public policy accountability, it appears that the role of responsible evaluation is gaining some degree of prominence in the policy-making arena. While it is not anticipated that future policy-making in corrections will be guided by an overriding concern for responsible evaluation, it seems that the role of such evaluation will become more integral to the policy-making process. The question remains whether or not evaluators will be able to meet this challenge. Previous inconclusive results of evaluations of correction programs have provided little in the way of meaningful policy direction. Nonetheless, it is possible that in the future the ambivalence that has facilitated politicized and often misguided policies in the past can be reduced. Policies informed by evaluations that specify what forms of intervention work best to alleviate particular social problems and forms of human misery while maintaining individual rights and freedom are elusive but not beyond our grasp.

1. Klein, M. "Deinstitutionalization and Diversion of Juvenile Offenders A Litany of Impediments." In N. Morris and M. Tonry (eds.) Crime and Justice. University of Chicago Press, 1979, pp. 147-148.

2. Lemert, E. M. "Diversion in Juvenile Justice: What Hath Been Wrought." Journal of Research in Crime and Delinquency 18 (1981):41-42.

3. Austin, J. and B. Krisberg. "Wider, Stronger, and Different Nets: The Dialectics of Criminal Justice Reforms." Journal of Research in Crime and Delinquency 18 (1981):169.

4. Polk, K. Youth Service Bureaus: The Record and Prospects. Eugene, Oregon: University of Oregon, 1981 Unpublished Mimeo.

5. Duxbury, E. Evaluation of Youth Service Bureaus. California Youth Authority, 1973.

6. Baron, R., F. Feeney and W. Thornton. "Preventing Delinquency Through Diversion." Federal Probation 37, 1 (1973):13-18; Thornton, W., E. Barrett and L. Musolf. The Sacramento County Probation Department 601 Diversion Project. Sacramento County Probation Department, 1972; Forward, J. R., M. Kirby and K. Wilson. Volunteer Intervention with Court-Diverted Juveniles. University of Colorado, 1974; Klein M. Alternative Dispositions for Juvenile Offenders. University of Southern California, 1975; Ku, R. and C. Blew. A University's Approach to Delinquency Project. U.S. Government Printing Office, 1977; and Quay, H. and C. Love. "The Effect of a Juvenile Diversion Program on Rearrest." Criminal Justice and Behavior 4 (1977):377-396.

7. The Evaluation of Juvenile Diversion Programs: Survey of Diversion Programs. California Youth Authority, November, 1975; The Evaluation of Juvenile Diversion Programs: First Annual Report. California Youth Authority, September, 1975; and The Evaluation of Juvenile Diversion Programs: Second Annual Report. California Youth Authority, September, 1976.

8. Bohnstedt, M., et al. The Evaluation of Juvenile Diversion. California Youth Authority, 1975.

9. Palmer, T. and R. Lewis. "A Differentiated Approach to Juvenile Diversion." Journal of Research in Crime and Delinquency 17, 2 (1980)":224.

10. Evaluation of the Juvenile Alternative Services Project. Florida Department of Human Resource Services, 1981.

11. Austin, J., B. Krisberg and W. Lawrence. Open Space, Community Detention, Pittsburgh-Antioch (AB 312): Diverting the Status Offender. Research Center West, National Council on Crime and Delinquency, 1978; Blomberg, T. "Diversion and Accelerated Social Control." The Journal of Criminal Law and Criminology 68, 2 (June, 1977):274-282; The Evaluation of Juvenile Diversion Programs: Survey of Diversion Programs. California Youth Authority, November, 1975; The Evaluation of Juvenile Diversion Programs: First Annual Report. California Youth Authority, September, 1975; The Evaluation of Juvenile Programs: Second Annual Report. California Youth Authority, September, 1976; Elliott, D. Diversion: A Study of Alternative Processing Practices. Center for Studies of Crime and Delinquency, NIMH, 1978; Klein, M. Alternative Dispositions for Juvenile Offenders. University of California, 1975; Klein, M. and K. Teilman. Pivotal Ingredients of Police Juvenile Diversion Programs. National Institute for Juvenile Justice and Delinquency Prevention, OJJDP/LEAA, 1976; Mattingly, J. and D. Katkin. "The Youth Service Bureau: A Re-invented Wheel?" San Francisco, California, 1975 Mimeo presented at the Society for the Study of Social Problems Meeting; Polk, 1981; Sarri, R. "Juvenile Aid Panels: An Alternative to Juvenile Court to Juvenile Court Processing." In P. Brantingham and T. Blomberg (eds.) Courts and Diversion: Policy and Operations Studies. Sage Publishing Company, 1979; Evaluation of the Juvenile Alternative Services Project. Florida Department of Human Resource Services, 1981.

12. California Youth Authority, see note 7.

13. Klein and Teilman, 1976.

14. Blomberg, T. "Widening the Net: An Anomoly in the Evaluation of Diversion Programs." In M. Klein and K. Tielman (eds.) Handbook of Criminal Justice Evaluation, Sage Publications, 1980, pp. 571-593.

15. Klein and Teilman, 1976; and Fishman, R. Criminal Recidivism in New York City: An Evaluation of the Impact of Rehabilitation and Diversion Services. Praeger, 1977.

16. Polk, 1981, p. 8.

17. For discussion see Blomberg, 1977, p. 280.

18. Deutscher, I. "Toward Avoiding the Goal Trap in Evaluation Research" In F. Cazo (ed.) Reading in Evaluation Research, 2nd Ed. Russel Sage Foundation, 1977.

19. National Evaluation Design for the Deinstitutionalization of Status Offender Program. U.S. Government Printing Office, 1976.

119

20. Chen, H. and P. Rossi. "The Multi-Goal, Theory Driven Approach to Evaluation: A Model Linking Basic and Applied Social Science." Social Forces 59, 1 (1980):106-122.

21. Chen and Rossi, pp. 109-112.

22. Palmer and Lewis, pp. 222-224.

23. Richardson, D., et al. "End of the Permissive Society." U.S. News and World Report, June 28, 1982, pp. 45-50.

24. "Hinckley Verdict Raises Cries for Insanity-Law Changes." Tallahassee Democrat, July 1, 1982.

25. "Candidate: Executive Smugglers." Tallahassee Democrat, July 4, 1982.

26. "Look Beyond Hinckley Verdict." Tallahassee Democrat, July 16, 1982.

27. Forst, M. L. Civil Commitment and Social Control. Lexington Books, 1978.

APPENDIX

RESEARCH METHODS

The research methods of this study were shaped by a concern which emphasizes the perspective of the organizational actors as a significant variable in understanding organizations. As a result, a primary research purpose was to describe, assess, and interpret the ongoing social interactions of North County's juvenile court personnel, and the perspectives that underlay those interactions. Schutz provides an appropriate summary of the theoretical underpinnings of this methodological approach:

> The observational field of the social scientist...has a specific meaning and relevance structure for the human beings living, acting, and thinking therein. By a series of commen-sense constructs they have pre-selected and pre-interpreted this world which they experience as the reality of their daily lives. It is these thought objects of theirs which determine their behavior by motivating it. The thought objects constructed by the social scientist, in order to grasp the social reality, have to be founded upon the thought objects constructed by the common-sense thinking of men, living their daily lives within their social world. [1]

The research for this study was carried out over a period of three years, prior to which the researcher spent two years as an employee of North County's juvenile court. The initial research procedure involved immersion in the workings of the juvenile court to the extent possible for a nonparticipant. The basic research methods employed were observations, interviews, and document analysis.

Observations were made of various interdepartmental meetings, budgetary planning meetings, and probation administrative meetings between the probation officer, juvenile court judges, county auditor, Board of Supervisor's representatives, and immediate administrative and supervisory staff. In addition, several regional meetings of the California Youth Authority and the California Council on Criminal Justice were observed. The intent of these observations was to understand the activity of North County's juvenile court system in terms of its internal affairs and its interaction with its significant environment.

Informal interviewing was the primary technique for gaining information on the juvenile court's perceived administrative problems, thinking, and action. In the initial research stages, a substantial amount of time was spent interviewing individuals with various roles in or ties to the juvenile court (i.e., juvenile court judges, probation personnel, local and state officials, and representatives of community organizations). A primary concern was to determine the kinds of internal problems, pressures, opportunities, and exchange relationships involved in moving the court toward particular modes of response and implementation of community correction reforms.

The interview mechanics involved covering specific subjects and questions in each session. However, the conversations were allowed to drift according to the particular familiarity or expertise of the respondent; the respondent was not asked to answer a fixed set of questions. This flexible interview procedure was particularly useful in the exploratory stages of the research work. It facilitated identification of the problems and helped the respondents' thinking more than dealing with hypothetical problems or issues that might have had relevance would have done. The informal interview data were controlled by cross-checking responses with other respondents and, whenever possible, with recorded or published materials.

Documentary analysis provided specific data regarding major court decisions and their overall system impact. Generally, problems, decisions, and policy determinations are recorded in some form. Court statistics reflect organizational activity related to youth-handling practices. However, gathering of direct proof is limited in most organizational settings. Instead, it is necessary to rely on indirect or partial indicators that together can provide data for accurate interpretations. Burton Clark provides a relevant appraisal of the formal methodological weakness of this form of organizational research. He states:

> An institutional study involves a search for the significant factors in a complex situation of social action. A strong point in such studies is their relevance to real problems and to significant aspects of behavior in a given situation. The orientations fruitful in such a search, however, naturally favor an emphasis upon discovery and less emphasis on close, immediate validation of research results. Moreover, the use of formal techniques is limited if the inquiry takes place within organizations, and the possibilities of clear and direct proof are thereby narrowed....The lack of immediate validation is defensible in that the ultimate validity of all research rests not in the tests of significance of the

moment, but upon whether the findings hang together with findings from other studies to produce a theoretical structure.[2]

It is important to recognize that this research, which resulted in a critical assessment of North County's juvenile court practices, by its very nature required considerable cooperation from various North County personnel. It is to be expected that research subjects who, in effect, make field research studies possible will react negatively to critical results, interpretations, and conclusions. Often the reaction is so negative that future researchers are denied access to the organization altogether. Whether such negative reactions can be avoided without compromising the research effort is a salient question. In a strict sense, negative responses of research subjects to critical research studies are unavoidable. Nonetheless, these negative reactions can be tempered by careful planning and clear and honest communication between the research subjects and the researcher. The research design and purposes need to be spelled out in the beginning and areas of concern clarified.

Normally, various reciprocal agreements are made before the research begins, and it is essential that the researcher live up to each of these agreements. For example, in the early stages of the North County study, it was agreed the county would remain anonomous and that before completion of the study, various county personnel would review a working draft for the purpose of identifying and correcting any factual errors in the findings. The researcher's interpretations of the findings were not subject to negotiation or debate. As it turned out, the only concern voiced about the study was related to the interpretations of the findings—the findings themselves were found to be correct. The probation officer summarized his concerns by stating, "The data are correct but what I don't like is the way you interpreted the data. You made me out to be an unprincipled empire builder." Even with the probation officer's closing reaction, the research agreements that were made were fulfilled. Entering upon research agreements and fulfilling them is within the control of the field researcher, whereas the reaction to the researcher's interpretations and conclusions on the basis of field research obviously is not.

NOTES

1.   Schutz, A.   "Concept and Theory Formation in the Social Sciences." <u>The Journal of Philosophy</u> 51 (April, 1954):266-267.

2.   Clark, D.   <u>Adult Education in Transition: A Study of Institutional Insecurity</u>.   University of California Press, 1958, p. 167.

BIBLIOGRAPHY

Akers, R. L. and R. Hawkins. Law and Control in Society. Englewood Cliffs, N.J.: Prentice-Hall, Inc., 1975.

Allen, F. A. The Borderland of Criminal Justice: Essays in Criminology. Chicago, Illinois: University of Chicago Press, 1964.

Arnold, M. "Juvenile Justice in Transition." UCLA Law Review 14 (1957):1144-1158.

Austin, J. and B. Krisberg. "Wider, Stronger, and Different Nets: The Dialectics of Criminal Justice Reforms." Journal of Research in Crime and Delinquency 18, 1 (1981):165-196.

Austin, J., B. Krisberg, and W. Lawrence. Open Space, Community Detention, Pittsburg-Antioch Diversion (AB 312): Diverting the Status Offender. Research Center West, National Council on Crime and Delinquency, 1978.

Baron, R. and F. Feeney. Juvenile Diversion Through Family Counseling, LEAA, NILECJ. Washington, D.C.: Government Printing Office, 1976.

Baron, R., F. Feeney, and W. Thornton. "Preventing Delinquency Through Diversion." Federal Probation 37, 1 (1973):13-18.

Behavior Research Institute. Work Plan National Evaluation of Diversion Programming. Boulder, Colorado, 1977.

Bellassai, J. "Pretrial Diversion: The First Decade in Retrospect." Pretrial Services Annual Journal (American Bar Association) (1978):13-16.

Berg, D. and D. Shichor. "Methodology and Theoretical Issues in Juvenile Diversion: Implications for Evaluation." Presented at the National Conference on Criminal Justice Evaluation, Washington, D.C., 1977. Mimeo.

Berger, D., M. Lipsey, L. Dennison, and J. Lange. "The Effectiveness of the Sheriff's Department's Juvenile Diversion Projects in Southeast Los Angeles County." Claremont, California: Claremont Graduate School, 1977. Mimeo.

Bidwell, C. E. "The School as a Formal Organization." In J. G. March (ed.), Handbook of Organizations. Chicago, Illinois: Rand McNally and Company, 1965.

Biel, M. Legal Issues and Characteristics of Pretrial Intervention Programs. Pretrial Intervention Service Center, American Bar Association, 1974.

Binder, A. "Diversion and the Justice System: Evaluating the Results." Irvine, California: University of California, n.d. Mimeo.

Binder, A., J. Monohan, and M. Newkirk. "Diversion from the Juvenile Justice System and the Prevention of Delinquency." In J. Monohan (ed.), Community Mental Health and the Criminal Justice System. New York: Pergamon Press, 1976.

Black, D. and A. Reiss. "Police Control of Juveniles." American Sociological Review 35 (1970):63-77.

Blomberg, T. G. "Diversion and Accelerated Social Control." The Journal of Criminal Law and Criminology 68, 2 (June, 1977):274-282.

Blomberg, T. G. "The Juvenile Court as an Organization and Decision-Making System." International Journal of Comparative and Applied Criminal Justice 1, 2 (1977):135-145.

Blomberg, T. G. "Diversion from Juvenile Court: A Review of the Evidence." In F. Faust and P. Brantingham (eds.), Juvenile Justice Philosophy, 2nd ed. Minneapolis, Minnesota: West Publishing Company, 1978.

Blomberg, T. G. "Widening the Net: An Anomaly in the Evaluation of Diversion Programs." In M. Klein and K. Teilmann (eds.), Handbook of Criminal Justice Evaluation. Beverly Hills, California: Sage Publishing Company, 1980.

Blomberg, T. G. and S. Caraballo. "Accelerated Family Intervention in Juvenile Justice." Crime and Delinquency 25, 4 (1979):497-502.

Blumberg, A. Criminal Justice. Chicago, Illinois: Quadrangle Books, 1967.

Board of Corrections. Institutions: Correctional Systems Study. Sacramento: State of California, 1971.

Bohnstedt, M., et al. The Evaluation of Juvenile Diversion. Sacramento: California Youth Authority, 1975.

Boole, K. L. The Juvenile Court: Its Origin, History, and Precedure. Berkeley, California: University of California, 1928. Unpublished doctoral dissertation.

Briar, S. and I. Piliavin. "Police Encounters with Juveniles." In R. Giallombardo (ed.), Juvenile Delinquency: A Book of Readings. New York: John Wiley and Sons, Inc., 1966.

Bureau of Criminal Statistics. Delinquency and Probation in California, annual reports. Sacramento: Department of Justice, 1957-1972.

Cahn, F. and V. Bary. Welfare Activities of Federal, State and Local Governments in California 1850-1934. Berkeley, California: University of California Press, 1936.

Caldwell, R. G. "The Juvenile Court: Its Development and Some Major Problems." Journal of Criminal Law, Criminology and Police Science 51 (1960):493-511.

California Law Relating to Youthful Offenders, Article 7. State Aid for Probation Services, Sections 1820-1826. Sacramento: Department of the Youth Authority, 1970.

California Probation, Parole, and Correctional Association. Probation Camp in California. Sacramento: Camps, Ranches and School Division, 1963.

California Statutes.
    1903 Chapter XLIII, Section 1. Sacramento: State of California.
    1909 Chapter 133, Section 1. Sacramento: State of California.
    1915 Chapter 631, Section 1 and 2. Sacramento: State of California.

California Welfare and Institutions Code, Article 15, Section 881. Sacramento: State of California, 1957.

California Youth Authority. The Evaluation of Juvenile Diversion Programs: Survey of Diversion Programs. Sacramento: State of California, November, 1975.

California Yourth Authority. The Evaluation of Juvenile Diversion Programs: First Annual Report. Sacramento: State of California, September, 1975.

California Youth Authority. The Evaluation of Juvenile Diversion Programs: Second Annual Report. Sacramento: State of California, September, 1976.

Canlis, M. W. "Tommorrow is Too Late." Youth Authority Quarterly 21 (Spring, 1968):9-16.

Carter, R. and G. Gilbert. An Evaluation Progress Report of the Alternative Routes Project. Los Angeles, California: University of Southern California Regional Research Institute in Social Welfare, 1973.

Carter, R. "The Diversion of Offenders." In G. G. Killinger and P. F. Cromwell, Jr. (eds.), Corrections in the Community: Alternatives to Imprisonment--Selected Readings, 2nd ed. St. Paul, Minnesota: West Publishing Company, 1978.

Carter, R. Evaluation of the Deinstitutionalization of Status Offenders Project Through the System Rates Methodology. Los Angeles, California: Social Science Research Institute, University of Southern California, 1978.

Carter, R. and M. W. Klein. Back on the Street: The Diversion of Juvenile Offenders. Englewood Cliffs, N. J.: Prentice-Hall, 1976.

Chen, H. T. and P. Rossi. "The Multi-Goal, Theory Driven Approach to Evaluation: A Model Linking Basic and Applied Social Science." Social Forces 59, 1 (1980):106-122.

Chute, C. "Fifty Years of the Juvenile Court." National Probation and Parole Association Yearbook (1949):1-20.

Cicourel, A. Measurement in Sociology. New York: The Free Press, 1964.

Cicourel, A. The Social Organization of Juvenile Justice. New York: John Wiley and Sons, Inc., 1968.

Clark, B. Adult Education in Transition: A Study of Institutional Insecurity. Berkeley, California: University of California Press, 1956.

Clark, B. The Open Door College: A Case Study. New York: McGraw-Hill Book Company, 1960.

Cohn, A. W. Decision-Making in the Administration of Probation Services: A Descriptive Study of the Probation Manager. Berkeley, California: University of California, 1972. Unpublished doctoral dissertation.

Cole, G. F. Criminal Justice: Law and Politics. North Scituate, Mass. and Belmont, California: Duxbury Press, 1972.

Cole, G. F. Politics and the Administration of Justice. Beverly Hills, California: Sage Publications, 1973.

Cressey, D. R. "Achievement of an Unstated Organizational Goal:
An Observation of Prisons." Pacific Sociological Review 1
(1958):43-49.

Cressey, D. and R. McDermott. Diversion from the Juvenile
Justice System. Ann Arbor, Michigan: National Assessment
of Juvenile Corrections, University of Michigan, 1973.

Crime and Delinquency. "Diversion in the Juvenile Justice
System: A Symposium." Vol. 22, 4 (1976).

Davis, G. "A Study of Adult Probation Violation Rates by Means
of the Cohort Approach." The Journal of Criminal Law and
Criminology and Police Science (March, 1964):86.

Dennison, L., L. Humphreys, and D. Wilson. "A Comparison:
Organization and Impact in Two Diversion Projects." Paper
presented at the meeting of the Pacific Sociological
Association, Victoria, B.C., 1975. Mimeo.

Deutsch, A. Our Rejected Children. Boston, Mass.: Little,
Brown and Company, 1947.

Deutscher, I. "Toward Avoiding the Goal Trap in Evaluation
Research." In F. Cazo (ed.), Reading in Evaluation Research,
2nd ed. New York: Russell Sage Foundation, 1977.

Dobbs, H. A. "In Defense of Juvenile Courts." Federal
Probation 13 (1949):24-29.

Dressler, D. Practice and Theory of Probation and Parole. New
York and London: Columbia University Press, 1959.

Dunford, F. W. "Police Diversion: An Illusion?" Criminology
15, 3 (1977):335-352.

Dunham, H. W. "The Juvenile Court: Contradictory Orientations
in Processing Offenders." Law and Contemporary Problems 23
(1958):512-525.

Duxbury, E. Evaluation of Youth Service Bureaus. Sacramento:
California Youth Authority, 1973.

Elliott, D. Evaluation of Youth Service Systems: FY 1973.
Boulder, Colorado: Behavior Research Evaluation Corporation,
1974.

Elliott, D. Diversion: A Study of Alternative Processing
Practices. Final report to the Center for Studies of Crime
and Delinquency, NIMH. Boulder, Colorado: Behavioral
Research Institute, 1978.

Elliott, D., F. Blanchard, and F. Dunford. The Long and Short Term Impact of Diversion Programs. Boulder, Colorado: Behavioral Research and Evaluation Corporation, 1976.

Emerson, R. M. Judging Delinquents: Context and Process in Juvenile Court. Chicago, Illinois: Aldine Publishing Company, 1969.

Empey, L. Alternatives to Incarceration. Washington, D.C.: U.S. Government Printing Office, 1967.

Empey, L. "Juvenile Justice Reform: Diversion, Due Process, and Deinstitutionalization." In L. Ohlin (ed.), Prisoners in America. Englewood Cliffs, N.J.: Prentice-Hall, 1973.

Erikson, K. Wayward Puritans: A Study in the Sociology of Deviance. New York: John Wiley and Sons, Inc., 1966.

Etzioni, Amitai. Modern Organizations. Englewood Cliffs, N.J.: Prentice-Hall, 1964.

Ewing, B. "Change and Continuity in Criminal Justice Research: A Perspective from NILECJ." Journal of Research in Crime and Delinquency 15, 2 (1978):266-278.

Ewing, B. "Responding to the Policymaker's Need for Research." In P. Brantingham and T. Blomberg (eds.), Courts and Diversion: Policy and Operations Studies. Beverly Hills, California: Sage Publishing Company, 1979.

Feeley, M. "Two Models of the Criminal Justice System: An Organizational Perspective." Law and Society Review 7 (1973):407-425.

Ferdinand, T. and E. Luchterhand. "Inner City Youth, the Police, the Juvenile Court and Justice." Social Problems 18 (1962):510-527.

Fishman, R. Criminal Recidivism in New York City: An Evaluation of the Impact of Rehabilitation and Diversion Services. New York: Praeger, 1977.

Forward, J. R., M. Kirby, and K. Wilson. Volunteer Intervention with Court-Diverted Juveniles. Boulder, Colorado: University of Colorado, 1974.

Forst, M. L. Civil Commitment and Social Control. Lexington, Mass.: Lexington Books, 1978.

Fox, S. "Juvenile Justice Reform: An Historical Perspective." Stanford Law Review 22 (1970):1187-1239.

Frazier, C. and R. Potter. "Diversion or Widening the Juvenile Justice Net: An Analysis of Effects of Decisions by Key Individuals." A paper presented a the American Society of Criminology meeting, San Francisco, California, November, 1980. Mimeo.

Freeman, H. E. and C. S. Sherwood. Social Research and Social Policy. Englewood Cliffs, N.J.: Prentice-Hall, 1970.

Galbraith, J. K. The New Industrial State. Boston, Mass.: Houghton Mifflin Company, 1967.

Galbraith, J. K. Economics and the Public Purpose. Boston, Mass.: Houghton Mifflin Company, 1973.

Garabedian, P. G. and D. C. Gibbons. Becoming Delinquent: Young Offenders and the Correctional System. Chicago, Illinois: Aldine Publishing Company, 1970.

Gibbons, D. and G. Blake. "Evaluating the Impact of Juvenile Diversion Programs." Crime and Delinquency 22, 4 (1976):411-420.

Gibbs, J. P. "Conceptions of Deviant Behavior: The Old and the New." Pacific Sociological Review 9 (1966)9-14.

Gold, M. and J. R. Williams. "National Study of the Aftermath of Apprehension." Prospectus 3 (1969):3.

Goldman, N. The Differential Selection of Juvenile Offenders for Court Appearance. Washington, D.C.: National Council on Crime and Delinquency, 1963.

Goldman, N. "The Differential Selection of Juvenile Offenders for Court Appearance." In William Chambliss (ed.), Crime and the Legal Process. New York: McGraw-Hill Company, 1969.

Goldstein, A. S. "The State and the Accused: Balance of Advantage in Criminal Procedures." Yale Law Journal 69 (1969):1149-1199.

Gore, W. J. Administrative Decision-Making: A Heuristic Model. New York: John Wiley and Sons, Inc., 1964.

Governor's Special Study Commission on Juvenile Justice Report. Sacramento: State of California, 1980.

Gulick, L. and L. Urwick (eds.). Papers on the Science of Administration. New York: Institute of Public Administration, 1937.

Gusfield, J. L. "Social Structure and Moral Reform: A Study of Women's Christian Temperance Union." American Journal of Sociology 61 (1955):221-232.

Gusfield, J. R. Symbolic Crusade: Status Politics and the American Temperance Movement. Urbana: University of Illinois Press, 1963.

Hackler, J. "Logical Reasoning Versus Unanticipated Consequences: Diversion Programs as an Illustration." Ottowa Law Review 8, 2 (Summer, 1976):285-289.

Hackler, J. The Prevention of Youthful Crime: The Great Stumble Forward. Toronto, Canada: Methuen Publications, 1978.

Hagan, J. "Extra-Legal Attributes and Criminal Sentencing: An Assessment of a Sociological Viewpoint." Law and Society Review 8 (1974):357-383.

Handler, J. F. "The Juvenile Court and the Adversary System: Problems of Function and Form." Wisconsin Law Review (1965):5-51.

Harlow, E. "Diversion from the Criminal Justice System." National Council on Crime and Delinquency, Crime and Delinquency Literature 2 (April 1970):136-164.

Hirschi, et al. "The Status of Self-Report Measures." In M. Klein and K. Teilmann (eds.), Handbook of Criminal Justice Evaluation. Beverly Hills, California: Sage Publishing Company.

Humphreys, L. and J. M. Carrier. Second Annual Evaluation Report: Pomona Valley Juvenile Diversion Project. Claremont, California: Pitzer College, 1976.

Hylton, J. Reintegrating the Offender: Assessing the Impact of Community Corrections. Washington, D.C.: University Press of America, 1981.

Jeffery, C. R. and I. A. Jeffery. "Prevention Through the Family." In W. E. Amos and C. F. Wellford (eds.), Delinquency Prevention Theory and Practice. New York: Prentice-Hall, Inc., 1967.

Kassenbaum, G. "Strategies for the Sociological Study of Criminal Correctional Systems." In R. W. Habenstein (ed.), Pathways to Data: Field Methods for Studying Ongoing Social Organizations. Chicago, Illinois: Aldine Publishing Co., 1970.

Kitsuse, J. "Societal Reactions to Deviant Behavior: Problems of Theory and Methods." Social Problems 9 (1963):247-256.

Klapmuts, N. Diversion from the Juvenile Justice System. Hackensack, N.J.: National Council on Crime and Delinquency, 1974.

Klein, M. "Labeling, Deterrence, and Recidivism: A Study of Police Dispositions of Juvenile Offenders." Social Problems 22, 2 (1974): 292-303.

Klein, M. Alternative Dispositions for Juvenile Offenders. Los Angeles, California: University of Southern California, 1975.

Klein, M. "On the Front End of the Juvenile Justice System." In R. Carter and M. Klein (eds.), Back on the Street: The Diversion of Juvenile Offenders. Englewood Cliffs, N. J.: Prentice-Hall, 1976.

Klein, M. and K. Teilmann. Pivotal Ingredients of Police Juvenile Diversion Programs. Washington, D.C.: National Institute for Juvenile Justice and Delinquency Prevention, OJJDP/LEAA, 1976.

Klein, M. and K. Teilmann (eds.). Handbook of Criminal Justice Evaluation. Beverly Hills, California: Sage Publishing Company, 1980.

Klein, M. "Deinstitutionalization and Diversion of Juvenile Offenders: A Litany of Impediments." In N. Morris and M. Tonry (eds.), Crime and Justice. Chicago, Illinois: University of Chicago Press, 1979

Kobetz, R. and B. Bosarge. "Diversion of Juvenile Offenders: An Overview." Juvenile Justice Administration (1973). National Association of Chiefs of Police.

Ku, R. and C. Blew. A University's Approach to Delinquency Prevention: The Adolescent Diversion Project. Washington, D.C.: U.S. Government Printing Office, 1977.

Kutchins, H. and S. Kutchins. "Pretrial Diversionary Programs: New Expansion of Law Enforcement Activity Camouflaged as Rehabilitation." Presented at the Pacific Sociological Association Meetings, Hawaii, 1975. Mimeo.

Lemert, E. M. "The Juvenile Court--Quest and Realities." In President's Commission on Law Enforcement and Administration of Justice. Task Force Report: Juvenile Delinquency and Youth Crime. Washington, D.C.: U.S. Government Printing Office, 1967.

Lemert, E. M. Social Action and Legal Change: Revolution Within the Juvenile Court. Chicago, Illinois: Aldine Publishing Company, 1970.

Lemert, E. M. "Diversion in Juvenile Justice: What Hath Been Wrought." Journal of Research in Crime and Delinquency 18 (1981):34-46.

Lemert, E. M. Instead of Court: Diversion in Juvenile Justice. Washington, D.C.: NIMH Center for Studies of Crime and Delinquency, U.S. Government Printing Office, 1971.

Lerman, P. Community Treatment and Social Control: A Critical Analysis of Juvenile Correctional Policy. Chicago, Illinois: University of Chicago Press, 1975.

Levine, S. and P. E. White. "Exchange as a Conceptual Framework for the Study of Interorganizational Relationships." In A. Etzioni (ed.), A Sociological Reader on Complex Organizations, 2nd ed. New York: Holt, Rinehart & Winston, Inc., 1969.

Lincoln, S. "Juvenile Referrals and Recidivism." In R. Carter and M. Klein (eds.), Back on the Street: The Diversion of Juvenile Offenders. Englewood Cliffs, N.J.: Prentice-Hall, 1976.

Lincoln, S. et al. "Recidivism Rates of Diverted Juvenile Offenders." Presented at the National Conference on Criminal Justice Evaluation, Washington, D.C., 1977. Mimeo.

Litterer, J. A. Organizations: Structure and Behavior. New York: John Wiley and Sons, Inc., 1963.

Lofland, J. Analyzing Social Settings. Belmont, California: Wadsworth Publishing Company, Inc., 1971.

Lou, H. H. Juvenile Courts in the United States. Chapel Hill, No. Carolina: University of North Carolina Press, 1927.

Mahoney, A. "The Effect of Labeling Upon Youths in the Juvenile Justice System: A Review of the Evidence." Law and Society Review 8 (1974):583-614.

March, J. G. and H. A. Simon. Organizations. New York: John Wiley and Sons, Inc., 1958.

Martinson, R. "What Works? Questions and Answers About Prison Reform." The Public Interest (1974):22-54.

Martinson, R. "California Research at the Crossroads." In M. Matlin (ed.), Rehabilitation, Recidivism, and Research. Hackensack, N.J.: National Council on Crime and Delinquency, 1976.

Mattingly, J. and D. Katkin. "The Youth Service Bureau: A Reinvented Wheel?" Presented at the Society for the Study of Social Problems Meeting, San Francisco, California, 1975. Mimeo.

McAlleenan, M., et al. Final Evaluation Report. The West San Gabriel Valley Juvenile Diversion Project. Los Angeles, California: Occidental College, 1977.

McEachern, A. W. "The Juvenile Probation System." American Behavioral Scientist 11, 3 (1968):1.

McKelvey, B. American Prisons: A History of Good Intentions. Montclair, N.J.: Patterson Smith, 1977.

Messinger, S. L. "Organizational Transformation: A Case Study of a Declining Social Movement." American Sociological Review 20 (1955):3-10.

Messinger, S. L. Strategies of Control. Los Angeles, California: University of California, 1969. Unpublished doctoral dissertation.

Messinger, S. L. "The Future of Punishment." In Crime and Justice In America. Del Mar, California: Publisher's Inc., 1977.

Messinger, S. L. Personal correspondence, 1980.

Messinger, S. L. "Punishments' Troubling Future." Chicago Tribune, December 16, 1977.

Michels, R. Political Parties: A Sociological Study of the Oligarchical Tendencies of Modern Democracy. New York: The Free Press, 1962.

Mileski, M. "Courtroom Encounters: An Observation Study of a Lower Criminal Court." Law and Society Review 5 (1971):473-538.

Miller, F. W., et al. The Juvenile Justice Process. Mineola, New York: Foundation Press, Inc., 1971.

Mohr, L. "Organizations, Decisions, and Courts." Law and Society Review 10 (1976):621-642.

Morris, N. The Future of Imprisonment. Chicago, Illinois: The University of Chicago Press, 1974.

Mouzelis, N. P. Organization and Bureaucracy: An Analysis of Modern Theories. Chicago, Illinois: Aldine Publishing Company, 1967.

Myer, M. and Associates. Environments and Organizations. San Francisco, California: Jossey-Bass Publisher, 1978.

National Evaluation Design for the Deinstitutionalization of Status Offender Program. Washington, D.C.: U.S. Government Printing Office, 1976.

National Pretrial Intervention Service Center. "Baltimore Pretrial Intervention Program." In Portfolio of Descriptive Profiles on Selected Pretrial Criminal Justice Intervention Programs. Washington, D.C.: American Bar Association, 1974.

Nejelski, P. "Diversion: The Promise and the Danger." Crime and Delinquency 22, 4 (1976):393-410.

New York Times. "Rise in Prisons' Populations Attributed to Tougher Laws." A.P., May 2, 1982.

New York Times. "U.S. Prison Roles Soar by Record 12 Percent." U.P.I., May 2, 1982.

Newman, D. J. The Decision as to Guilt or Innocence. American Bar Foundation, 1962.

Newman, G. G. (ed.) Children in the Courts: The Question of Representation. Ann Arbor, Michigan: Institute of Continuing Legal Education, University of Michigan, 1967.

Nonet, P. Administrative Justice: Advocacy and Change in Government Agencies. New York: Russell Sage Foundation, 1969.

Norman, Sherwood. The Youth Service Bureau: A Brief Description for Five Current Programs. New York: National Council on Crime and Delinquency, 1970.

North County Annual Probation Reports. North County: 1940 to
1972.

O'Brien, K. and M. Marcus. Juvenile Diversion: A Selected
Bibliography. U.S. Department of Justice, LEAA/NILECJ.
Washington, D.C.: U.S. Government Printing Office, 1976.

Olsen, M. E. The Process of Social Organization. New York:
Holt, Rinehart & Winston, Inc., 1968.

Packer, H. L. "Two Models of the Criminal Process." University
of Pennsylvania Law Review 113 (1964):1-68.

Packer, H. L. The Limits of the Criminal Sanction. Stanford,
California: Stanford University Press, 1968.

Palmer, T. "Martinson Revisited." Crime and Delinquency.
(1976):178-179.

Palmer, T. and R. Lewis. "A Differentiated Approach to Juvenile
Diversion." Journal of Research in Crime and Delinquency 17,
2 (1980):209-229.

Paternoster, R., G. Waldo, T. Chiricos, and L. Anderson. "The
Stigma of Diversion: Labeling in the Juvenile Justice
System." In P. Brantingham and T. Blomberg (eds.), Courts
and Diversion: Policy and Operations Studies. Beverly Hills,
California: Sage Publishing Company, 1979.

Perlman, R. and A. Gurin. Community Organization and Social
Planning. New York: John Wiley and Sons, Inc., 1972.

Perrow, C. Organizational Analysis: A Sociological View.
Belmont, California: Brooks/Cole Publishing Company, 1970.

Perrow, C. Complex Organizations: A Critical Essay. Glenview,
Illinois: Scott, Foresman and Company, 1972.

Pezman, T. L. Untwisting the Twisted. Sacramento: Probation
Camps, Ranches, and Schools, California Probation, Parole and
Correctional Division, July, 1963.

Piliavin, I. and S. Briar. "Police Encounters with Juveniles."
American Journal of Sociology 70 (1964):206-214.

Piliavan, I. and C. Werthman. "Gang Members and the Police."
In D. Bordua (ed.), The Police: Six Sociological Essays.
New York: John Wiley and Sons, Inc., 1967.

Platt, A. M. The Child Savers. Chicago and London: The
University of Chicago Press, 1969.

Platt, A. M. "The Triumph of Benevolence: The Origins of the Juvenile Justice System in the United States." In A. Blumberg (ed.), Introduction to Criminology. New York: Random House, 1972.

Polk, K. "Delinquency Prevention and the Youth Service Bureau." Criminal Law Bulletin 7 (1971):490-529.

Polk, K. "Youth Service Bureaus: The Record and Prospects." Eugene, Oregon: University of Oregon, 1981. Mimeo.

President's Commission on Law Enforcement and Administration of Justice. Task Force Report: Juvenile Delinquency and Youth Crime. Washington, D.C.: U.S. Government Printing Office, 1967.

Preston School of Industry. Fourth Biennial Report of the Board of Trustees, 1898-1900. Sacramento: State of California.

Public Systems, Inc. California Correctional System Intake Study. Sunnyvale, California, 1974.

Quay, H. C. and C. T. Love. "The Effect of a Juvenile Diversion Program on Rearrest." Criminal Justice and Behavior 4 (1977):377-396.

Reckless, W. The Crime Problem. New York: Appleton Century Crots, 1971.

Renn, D. E. "The Right to Treatment and the Juvenile." Crime and Delinquency 19 (1973):477-484.

Richardson, D., et al. "End of the Permissive Society." U.S. News and World Report, June 28, 1982.

Rosenheim, M. Justice for the Child: A Juvenile Court in Transition. New York: The Free Press of Glencoe, 1962.

Rosenheim, M. "Youth Service Bureaus: A Concept in Search of Definition." Juvenile Court Judges Journal 20 (Summer, 1969):69-74.

Ross, R. R. and P. Gendreau (eds.). Effective Correctional Treatment. Toronto, Canada: Butterworths, 1980.

Rothman, D. J. The Discovery of the Asylum. Boston and Toronto: Little, Brown and Company, 1971.

Rutherford, A. and O. Bengur. Community-Based Alternatives to Juvenile Incarceration. U.S. Department of Justice, LEAA/NILECJ. Washington, D.C.: U.S. Government Printing Office, 1976.

Rutherford, A. and R. McDermott. Juvenile Diversion. U.S. Department of Justice, LEAA/NILECJ. Washington, D.C.: U.S. Government Printing Office, 1976.

Sarri, R. "Juvenile Aid Panels: An Alternative to Juvenile Court Processing." In P. Brantingham and T. Blomberg (eds.), Courts and Diversion: Policy and Operations Studies. Beverly Hills, California: Sage Publishing Company, 1979.

Sarri, R. and P. Isenstadt. Remarks presented at the Hearings of the House of Representatives Select Committee on Crime, April 18, 1973. Ann Arbor, Michigan: NAJC, The University of Michigan, n.d.

Sarri, R. and R. Vinter. "Justice for Whom? Varieties of Juvenile Correctional Approaches." In M. Klein (ed.), The Juvenile Justice System. Beverly Hills, California: Sage Publishing Company, 1976.

Satir, V. Conjoint Family Therapy. Palo Alto, California: Science and Behavior Books, Inc., 1967.

Schlossman, S. Love and the American Delinquent: The Theory and Practice of "Progressive" Juvenile Justice, 1825-1920. Chicago, Illinois: University of Chicago Press, 1977.

Schur, E. Labeling Deviant Behavior: Its Sociological Implications. New York: Harper and Row, 1971.

Schur, E. Radical Non-Intervention: Rethinking the Delinquency Problem. Englewood Cliffs, N.J.: Prentice-Hall, Inc., 1973.

Scott, W. R. "Field Methods in the Study of Organization." In J. G. March (ed.), Handbook of Organizations. Chicago, Illinois: Rand McNally and Company, 1965.

Schutz, A. "Concept and Theory Formation in the Social Sciences." The Journal of Philosophy 51 (April, 1954):266-267.

Selznick, P. "Foundations of a Theory of Organization." American Sociological Review 13 (1948):25-35.

Selznick, P. TVA and the Grass Roots. New York: Harper and Row, Inc., 1966.

Selznick, P. Leadership in Administration. Evanston, Illinois: Row Peterson, 1957.

Selznick, P. Law, Society and Industrial Justice. New York: Russell Sage Foundation, 1969.

Sherdan, W. H. "Juveniles Who Commit Noncriminal Acts: Why Treat in a Correctional System?" Federal Probation 31 (1967):26-36.

Simon, H. A. Administrative Behavior: A Study of Decision-Making Processes in Administrative Organization. New York: The Free Press, 1965.

Skolnick, J. "The Sociology of Law in America: Overview and Trends." Law and Society (Summer Supplement, 1965):4-39.

Skolnick, J. Justice Without Trial: Law Enforcement in Democratic Society. New York: John Wiley and Sons, Inc., 1966.

Smith, R. L. Youth and Correction: An Institutional Analysis of the California Youth Authority. Berkeley, California: University of California, 1955. Unpublished master's thesis.

Smith, R. L. A Quiet Revolution: Probation Subsidy. U.S. Department of Health, Education and Welfare. Washington, D.C.: DHEW Publication No. (SRS) 72-26011, 1971.

Spergel, I. A. Community Problem Solving: The Delinquency Example. Chicago, Illinois: The University of Chicago Press, 1969.

Spergel, I. A. Community Problem Solving: Studies in Constraint. Beverly Hills and London: Sage Publications, 1972.

Spitzer, S. Labeling and Deviant Behavior: A Study of Imputation and Reaction in the Definition of Self. Bloomington, Indiana: Indiana University 1971. Unpublished doctoral dissertation.

State of Florida. Evaluation of the Juvenile Alternative Service Project. Tallahassee: Department of Human Resource Services, 1981.

Street, D., R. Vinter and C. Perrow. Organizations for Treatment. New York: The Free Press, 1966.

Sudnow, D. "Normal Crimes: Sociological Features of the Penal Code in a Public Defender Office." Social Problems 12 (1965):255-275.

Sudnow, D. "The Public Defender." In R. D. Schwartz and J. Skolnick (eds.), Society and the Legal Order. New York: Basic Books, Inc., 1970.

Tallahassee Democrat. "Hinckley Verdict Raises Cries for Insanity-Law Changes." July 1, 1982.

Tallahassee Democrat. "Candidate: Execute Smugglers." July 4, 1982.

Tallahassee Democrat. "Look Beyond Hinckley Verdict." July 16, 1982.

Tappan, P. W. Delinquent Girls in Court. New York: Columbia University Press, 1947.

Taylor, F. W. Scientific Management. New York: Harper and Row, 1911.

Teeters, N. K. and J. O. Reinneman. The Challenge of Delinquency. New York: Prentice-Hall, Inc., 1950.

Terry, R. "Discrimination in the Handling of Juvenile Offenders by Social Control Agencies." Journal of Research in Crime and Delinquency 4 (1967):218-230.

Thomas, C. W. and C. M. Sieverdes. "Juvenile Court Intake: An Analysis of Discretionary Decision-Making." Criminology 12 (1975):413-432.

Thompson, J. D. Organization in Action. New York: McGraw-Hill Book Company, 1967.

Thompson, J. D. and W. J. McEwen. "Organizational Goals and Environment." In A. Etzioni (ed.), A Sociological Reader on Complex Organizations, 2nd ed. New York: Holt, Rinehart and Winston, Inc., 1969.

Thornberry, T. Punishment and Crime: The Effect of Legal Dispositions on Subsequent Criminal Behavior. Philadelphia, Pennsylvania: University of Pennsylvania, 1971. Unpublished doctoral dissertation.

Thornberry, T. "Race, Socioeconomic Status and Sentencing in the Juvenile Justice System." Journal of Criminal Law and Criminology 64 (1973):90-98.

Thornton, W., E. Barrett, and L. Musolf. The Sacramento County Probation Department 601 Diversion Project. Sacramento: Sacramento County Probation Department, 1972.

Tittle, C. "Book Review of R. Fishman (1977) Criminal Recidivism in New York City: An Evaluation of the Impact of Rehabilitation and Diversion Services." Contemporary Sociology 8, 3 (1979):403-404.

Toby, J. "The Differential Impact of Family Disorganization." American Sociological Review (October, 1957):505-512.

Transactions of the Commonwealth Club of California, Vol. V. San Francisco, California, 1910.

Underwood, W. A. "California's Youth Service Bueraus." Youth Authority Quarterly (Winter, 1969):27-33.

Vaughn, R. "A Century of County Camps." Youth Authority Quarterly 17, 3 (Fall, 1964):26-31.

Vinter, R.D. "The Juvenile Court as an Institution." In President's Commission on Law Enforcement and Administration of Justice. Task Force Report: Juvenile Delinquency and Youth Crime. Washington, D.C.: U.S. Government Printing Office, 1967.

Vinter, R. D., et al. Juvenile Corrections in the States: Residential Programs and Deinstitutionalization. A Preliminary Report. Ann Arbor, Michigan: National Assessment of Juvenile Corrections, University of Michigan, 1975.

Vorenberg, E. and J. Vorenberg. "Early Diversion From the Criminal Justice System: Practice in Search of Theory." In L. Ohlin (ed.), Prisoners in America. Englewood Cliffs, N.J.: Prentice-Hall, 1973.

Ward, R. H. "The Labeling Theory: A Critical Analysis." Criminology: An Interdisciplinary Journal 9 (August, 1971):268-290.

Warren, M. "The Case for Differential Treatment of Delinquents." In H. L. Voss (ed.), Society, Delinquency and Delinquent Behavior. Boston, Mass.: Little, Brown and Company, 1970.

Weber, M. The Theory of Social and Economic Organizations. A. M. Anderson and T. Parsons (trans.) and T. Parsons (ed.). New York: The Free Press of Glencoe, 1947.

Wellford, C. "Labeling Theory and Criminology: An Assessment." _Social Problems_ 22 (1975):332-345.

Wheeler, S. (ed.). _Controlling Delinquents._ New York: John Wiley and Sons, Inc., 1968.

White, S. and S. Krislov (eds.). _Understanding Crime: An Evaluation of the National Institute of Law Enforcement and Criminal Justice._ Washington, D.C.: National Academy of Sciences, 1977.

Wilkins, L. T. _Evaluation of Penal Measures._ New York: Random House, Inc., 1969.

Williams, J. and M. Gold. "From Delinquent Behaviors to Official Delinquency." _Social Problems_ 20 (1972):209-227.

Wolfgang, M. E., R. M. Figlio and T. Sellin. _Delinquency in a Birth Cohort._ Chicago, Illinois: University of Chicago Press, 1972.

Wolin, S. S. "A Critique of Organizational Theories." In A Etzioni (ed.), _A Sociological Reader on Complex Organizations_, 2nd ed. New York: Holt, Rinehart and Winston, Inc., 1969.

Youth Services Bueraus. _Standards and Guidelines._ Sacramento: California Delinquency Prevention Commission, October, 1968.

Zald, M. N. "The Correctional Institution for Juvenile Offenders: An Analysis of Organizational 'Character'." _Social Problems_ 8 (1960):57-67.